Dear Chris,

I pray when this book reaches your hands you are in a peaceful place where you can find Solace and Quietness, to Spend Some time with GOD + You! With April 2010 right around the corner as you embark on one of the most memorable moments in your life "Mommy in Training" conference #1, Enjoy the Journey and the moments getting there! Don't stress— Just continue to Ask GOD To carry you through!

Thank you for your friendship and Dedication— You are a True sister in the Lord To Me And I ♡ U for that! Continue on striving to be all that you can be for GOD! All your HARD WORK AND efforts will Pay off at the "Golden Gates of Heaven!" Love Ya, Tracy ☺

"I realized that if I make time to nourish myself, I have more energy to praise God, play with my children and still have love left over for my husband at the end of the day. The dishes and laundry were miraculously done too!"—*Wendy*

"A MUST HAVE for moms everywhere! Lisa speaks from experience and relates to you both as a friend and a mentor."—*Lisa J.*

"If I had ten thumbs—they'd all be up! There is so much insight and practical ideas inside this book one can read it over and over again and find new ideas every time. Just when I thought it couldn't be done, you've shown me how to get more time out of my hectic days."—*Kelly*

"Lisa helps tired, burned-out mommies to find easy and fun ways to take care of ourselves so that we can come back to our families refreshed and ready to love them the way God wants us to."—*Lesley*

"I love the humor. It feels like I am getting advice from an old friend who really knows me! I can't believe how easily I am finding more time to spend with God and at the same time, improving the care I am giving to my family."—*Bethany*

"I appreciate 'bite sized' pieces. I love being able to choose and implement one or two ideas at a time."—*Cindy*

"Packed with a loaded picnic basket of tips and ideas to help overworked, overstressed, and overtired mothers."—*Amey*

"The me in mommy was exhausted and now I feel recharged!"—*Joi*

"The Rest Stops are pure treasure. These are simple ideas that can fit into a busy day. That is what all of those other books are missing."—*Hollie*

"My whole family thanks you!"—*Jamie*

"After reading this book and implementing a few of the suggestions, I feel like I fell in love with my family and being a Mom all over again!"—*Michelle*

"I feel you have taught me how to put the fuel back in my 'mommy tank'"—*Danielle*

"I think that so many mothers believe that being 'martyr mom' will somehow benefit their family, but for me it has proven to be fruitless and frustrating. Thank you so very much for listening to the voice of God to help the moms who care for His little ones."—*Evin*

"I am finally taking the time to nourish my spirit and in doing so, it's not only blessed me, but my family as well."—*Holly*

"It's amazing how a few minor adjustments on running a home can save you so much time!"—*Wade*

"I plan to read it often and use the Rest Stops until my children are in college!—*Sondra*

"Thanks to Lisa's practical tips on prayer, I have been able to expand my prayer time throughout the day!"—*Candace*

"I have realized that I do not need to be perfect to be happy. I have also been reminded how true it is that having our Heavenly Father as #1 in our lives makes all the difference."—*Ivonne*

"It is amazingly freeing to finally have permission to take care of myself. There is more to motherhood than raising my children. I must also take care of myself and my relationship with Christ."—*Rachelle*

"This book is filled with tips that even our tight budget can work with. I am feeling more energized and ready to make some positive changes, for ME and ultimately for my family that I love dearly!"—*Shirley*

"As a busy mom, I don't even have time to think of ways to make my life easier. With the Rest Stops, half the work is done for me. I truly believe this is more than just a helpful book—its life-changing."—*Lisa R.*

"By learning to rest and receive, meal times are more enjoyable, playtime is more frequent and family time is a true blessing."—*Danielle*

"I have been so overwhelmed lately that I am at the point of tears daily. I am cranky with my children and husband and feel tremendous guilt that I can't do everything I expect myself to do. This book not only lets me know I am not alone, but that there is light at the end of the tunnel and that I can enjoy being a mommy again."—*Star*

"All of the scripture, personal reflections and 'rest stops' Lisa gives are the 'ingredients' that I will add each day so my family can enjoy a healthy, hearty serving of 'mommy.'"—*Lisa S.*

"Lisa spelled out for me what I was desperately trying to figure out myself—me time!!!"—*Amy*

"We can't give away what we don't have. Lisa helped me to have an overflowing tank so that I may have so much more to give to my family than I ever thought possible. Just by implementing a couple of these simple strategies, my life seems so much more organized, simpler, and more balanced. Not only do I now have ways of taking care of 'me,' but I'm now able to give more to my family as a result! What an awesome feeling!"—*Kathy*

taking care of the
me
in mommy

becoming a
better mom —
spirit,
body &
soul

Lisa Whelchel

THOMAS NELSON
Since 1798

NASHVILLE DALLAS MEXICO CITY RIO DE JANEIRO BEIJING

Published in Nashville, Tennessee, by Thomas Nelson. Thomas Nelson is a trademark of Thomas Nelson, Inc.

Thomas Nelson, Inc. books may be purchased in bulk for educational, business, fund-raising, or sales promotional use. For information, please e-mail SpecialMarkets@ThomasNelson.com.

Unless otherwise indicated, Scripture quotations are taken from The Holy Bible, English Standard Version. © 2001 by Crossway Bibles, a division of Good News Publishers. Used by permission. All rights reserved.

Other Scripture quotations are taken from the following sources: The Holy Bible, New International Version® (NIV®). © 1973, 1978, 1984 by International Bible Society. Used by permission of Zondervan. All rights reserved. The New King James Version® (NKJV®). © 1982 by Thomas Nelson, Inc. Used by permission. All rights reserved. The Holy Bible, New Living Translation® (NLT®). © 1996. Used by permission of Tyndale House Publishers, Inc., Wheaton, Illinois 60189. All rights reserved. The New Century Version® (NCV®). © 1987, 1988, 1991 by Thomas Nelson, Inc. Used by permission. All rights reserved. American Standard Version (ASV). Public domain.

Cover Design: Brand Navigation, www.brandnavigation.com
Interior Design: Inside Out Design & Typesetting

ISBN 978-1-59145-435-9 (hc)
ISBN 978-0-7852-8929-6 (tp)

Printed in the United States of America
07 08 09 10 11 RRD 8 7 6 5 4 3

I happily dedicate this book to

The Good Medicine Club

Andrea, Connie, Deb, Denise, Sallie, Shawn, and Valerie

We learned how to be mommies together and

you, my lifelong friends, will forever be—

The Original MomTime Group!

Two are better than one,

because they have a good return for their work:

If one falls down, his friend can help him up.

But pity the man who falls and has no one to help him up!

Ecclesiastes 4:9–10 NIV

C ontents

Contents

Contents

cknowledgments

"Freely you have received, freely give."
Matthew 10:8 NKJV

I have received far more than I could ever give. My life, and this book, are better because of the people named here and their willingness to share their gifts with me so that I could pass them on to you.

Steve, Tucker, Haven, and Clancy—Thank you for not caring whether I'm an actress, author, butcher, baker, or candlestick maker. For loving me whether I'm frumpy, grumpy, together, or losin' it. To you, I'm simply Mom (and wife.) If that is enough for you, then it is enough for me. I love you.

Integrity Publishers and Laura Minchew—Thank you for your patience when I have taken care of the "me" in this mommy when I should have been writing. I am thrilled for the opportunity to partner with a publisher with such impeccable integrity and reputation. It is an honor.

Jennifer Stair—Thank you for the fabulous job you performed as editor. Each comment and note you sent to me was full of wisdom and obvious love for every mom who might read this book.

acknowledgments

Gladys Marie Brown—Thank you for, once again, coming to my rescue. I don't know what I would have done if you hadn't helped me sort through, organize, and put together the hundreds of Rest Stop ideas. You are one amazing administrator and editor.

Melanie Hill—Thank you for jumping in at the first utterance of "Help!" and researching the last-minute touches. You are a true friend.

Ron Smith—Thank you for your commitment to me and this ministry to moms. Underneath that thick manager skin is a tender heart for God and His work. (I knew it was there all along.)

E-Letter Moms—Thanks so much to the countless Web site friends who responded to my e-letter by sending so many practical, realistic, and "brilliant ideas." I am especially grateful to Kym Carter for organizing the "Mom/Me" focus group which provided invaluable insight in the beginning.

Cyber Prayer Warriors—Thank you for your faithfulness to lift up this book over the past two years. Your prayers have prevailed, and I will praise the Lord for the gift of your devoted friendship.

Maggie Murphy—Thank you for doing all the stuff I don't want to do. How in the world did we ever get along without you? You are an angel.

Al and Tracie Denson—Thank you again and again for opening up your bunkhouse as a place to retreat and write. You make it so easy to ask for help.

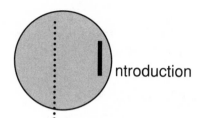 ntroduction

Taking Care of Yourself

*W*ouldn't you love to have an hour to spend time with the Lord, play a game with your kids, talk to your husband, or hang out with a girlfriend? As moms, we get so busy *doing* and *giving* that we often don't take time to *rest* and *receive*.

We've bought into the worldview that we can have it all and then believed the self-talk that insists, "If I don't do it, it won't get done." Isn't it ironic that at the same time we are feeling more and more driven, we are usually running on empty or, at the very least, on exhaust fumes? (You know what I mean: we're either "exhausted" or "fuming.") We are worn out trying to do it all. No wonder there is such an epidemic of mom burnout!

Trust me, I'm writing from personal experience here. I was recently reading through some of my old journals from when my children were smaller and came across the following paragraphs I thought you might appreciate:

> *I'm very sleepy, I'm tired of taking care of sick kids, and Tucker seems out of control. All boundaries and rules have*

disintegrated because he's sick. I have no idea when Steve will be home. And there are 4 hours and 15 minutes before I can put the first one to bed. There's a sneak preview of a movie tonight that I've wanted to see. But I can't go. Tucker just informed me that his ear hurts really badly. The doctor's office is closed. I feel fat and unmotivated. And there's nothing good to eat in this house. Other than that it's been a great day. Except for the big argument Steve and I had before he left this morning.

And . . .

*I'm sooooo tired. Not really physically, although that, too. Mostly, emotionally stressed. Just in case 5 years from now I forget, let me just now state for the record. **Raising three preschoolers is exhausting!** I decided this morning not to count on doing anything for myself. That means no treadmill, no bath, no cleaning, no computer, etc.*

Yes, I, too, thought the answer was doing less for me and more for them. I just ended up unhealthy, stinky, messy, and out of touch with the world beyond my little house of munchkins.

I understand there are seasons in a mother's life, and some ages require more self-sacrifice than others. By all means, lay down your life for your children, especially when they are small and are dependent on you for just about everything.

I can just tell you from firsthand knowledge, whenever I did take a bit of time for myself, whether it was coffee with my mom, a women's luncheon at church, or my annual spring pedicure, I always came home more in love with my family than when I left.

Maybe it is the adage, *Absence makes the heart grow fonder.* I don't know. I think it has more to do with the fact that we do love our families so desperately, but occasionally the exhaustion and busyness overwhelms us and we lose sight of this truth. When we pull away from the mayhem, regroup, and refresh, we come back with more to give than if we stayed in the rut, running around in circles, being the "good mom."

Moms give and give. But if you never learn to receive, then you have nothing left to give. If you won't take time for yourself, then take time for yourself for your family. By filling up your tank regularly, you will have the energy to drive your children to all their activities, drive your husband wild with desire, drive back the enemy in prayer, and drive a hard bargain at the latest clearance sale. You can't do any of these things if you are broken down and out of gas on the side of the road.

It is time to recharge and refuel. The first thing to do is plug into the Power Source and jump-start your day. Jesus says, "Whoever abides in me and I in him, he it is that bears much fruit, for apart from me you can do nothing" (John 15:5). If we don't want to spend our days running around in circles, feeling like we're heading nowhere and accomplishing nothing, then we need to stay connected to Jesus.

In John 15, after Jesus instructs us to abide in Him, He tells us why: "that my joy may be in you, and that your joy may be full" (v. 11). Jesus is the genesis of joy. He loves it when we laugh. It makes Him happy to see us happy. He doesn't want us running on empty; He wants our joy to be full.

So what fills you up? What do you enjoy doing? Does a hot bubble bath with candles sound heavenly to you? Do you desire a quiet dinner out with your husband? Or perhaps you'd love to have a whole day to wait on the Lord, linger in the Word, and tarry in prayer. Is your idea of a good time snuggling up with a book and some hot tea? Then do it. Receive it! Then return refueled and ready to give to your family out of the overflow.

I know what you're saying: "That sounds great, but where am I going to find the time?" By pulling over to the side of the road—this time on purpose. At the end of each brief chapter in this book, there will be a Rest Stop. This is the point in the journey when you can relax, replenish, refresh, receive, reorganize, rekindle, renew, and any other "re-" word you can think of.

Every part of you—body, soul, and spirit—needs nourishment, and I have packed a whole picnic basket full of realistic tips and ideas that I can't wait to open up and share with you. To me, the Rest Stops are the heart of this book. If you discover and apply even a couple of practical ideas that change your life and, subsequently, your family's lives, then I will be happy. I'll teach you how to "Scripture primp," worship while vacuuming, journal to your mother-in-law, and memorize Scripture every time you grab a drink out of the fridge. I'll show you how to find lost time with easy housecleaning tips and simple organizational skills. I'll share time-saving cooking plans and money-saving budget suggestions.

Now the question is, what are you going to do with all of this extra time on your hands? You are going to start by taking care of the "me" in mommy. That's right: you are going to invest it in yourself. I can't stress this enough—it is not selfish, wrong, or unworthy to take care of yourself, so you can better take care of your family.

As moms and Christians, we usually feel guilty about thinking of ourselves. Our instinct as mothers is to give without expectation of receiving, and we are wisely taught as Christians that the best way to look out for ourselves is not to. So, as a Christian mom, you probably are feeling guilty for even picking this book up, much less, reading this far into the Introduction. Remember, conviction is healthy; guilt is not. Allow me to share some truth from God's Word, and hopefully it will set you free from unhealthy guilt.

This book is not about "looking out for number one." It is about making Jesus number one in your life and believing Him when He says, "Seek first [God's] kingdom and his righteousness, and all these things will be given to you as well" (Matthew 6:33 NIV). "All these things" aren't bad desires; they are good things like food and clothing. What would make them bad is if we seek the gifts rather than the Giver.

What's so cool is the fact that God loves to give good gifts. "If you then, who are evil, know how to give good gifts to your children, how much more will your Father who is in heaven give good things to those who ask him!" (Matthew 7:11). So in the end, we get both: the Giver and His gifts.

In his book *Desiring God*, pastor John Piper writes, "God is most glorified in us when we are most satisfied in Him. This is the best news in the world! God's passion to be glorified and my passion to be satisfied are not at odds."[1] I think we can all agree on the high priority of doing "spiritual" things like Bible study and prayer. And yes, God is glorified when we serve Him by taking care of our children and ministering to others. Yet God is no less glorified when we enjoy a good meal, read an interesting book, or indulge in stimulating conversation.

There are a lot of right and good and necessary books written about the importance of nourishing our spirits to receive the strength we need for the tasks of the day. But God created us spirit, body, and soul. As the apostle Paul says, "May *your whole spirit and soul and body* be kept blameless at the coming of our Lord Jesus Christ" (1 Thessalonians 5:23; emphasis added).

I've organized the book into three sections with this scripture in mind: spirit, body, and soul. For easy reference, I'll use the following definitions from the original Greek language, written by much more worthy resources than myself:

Spirit (pneuma)—Man's immaterial nature, which enables him to communicate with God, who is also spirit.[2]

Body (soma)— the living body.[3]

Soul (psuche)—The part of man that knows, reasons, wills, desires, and feels. It refers to the will, the emotions, and the reason. With the physical body, man has world-consciousness, with the soul he has self-consciousness, and with the spirit he has God-consciousness.[4]

The following chapters will be full of encouragement and realistic ways for you, as a busy mom, to find time to sit at the feet of Jesus and receive the strength to continue pouring out your life for your family. There will also be tons of tips on ways to nurture your body and nourish your soul.

I have an idea. Why don't you read the next chapter while soaking in a hot bath? I'm serious. Run a hot bubble bath, gather some candles, and place them all around the rim. Maybe even bring a boom box into the bathroom and play some soothing music.

If you can't take a bath right this minute, then think ahead and plan a time in the near future when you can. Start taking care of the "me" in mommy right away. Trust me, you'll be a better mommy after a relaxing bath. That may sound crazy, but it is true. We really can take better care of our families when we start taking better care of ourselves. Start running that bathwater now!

Rest Stop

Let's Have a Picnic

*J*n the Introduction, I mentioned that I "packed a whole picnic basket full of realistic tips and ideas that I can't wait to open up and share with you" in the Rest Stops. Let's take this picnic basket analogy a bit further.

First of all, imagine that the basket is huge, too big for one person to carry. Now peek inside and notice that I've packed enough for an army. There is every kind of sandwich imaginable: turkey, ham, PB&J, club, panini, croissant, liverwurst, pickles and cheese, and my favorite, sugar and butter on white bread. Yes, I was born way back before our moms knew to be health conscious.

Dig around a bit, and you will discover that I've also gone overboard on the snacks. You can find potato chips of all kinds: BBQ, sour cream, vinegar, pickle, ranch, jalapeno, guacamole, wavy, baked, natural, even vegetable chips. Rest assured, I didn't forget the Cheetos®, Fritos®, Doritos®, Bugles®, Sun Chips®, and pork rinds.

Have a sweet tooth? Not for long. I've loaded up Twinkies®, ding dongs, Chips Ahoy®, Milk Duds®, animal crackers, Cracker Jacks®, M&Ms®, Red Vines®, and on and on and on. Don't worry, I also threw in a bountiful assortment of fruits and vegetables. I also brought so many drinks they wouldn't fit into the picnic basket, so don't forget to grab the ice chest as you pull into the first Rest Stop.

Now let me ask you a question. If I handed this picnic basket to you, would you look inside and say to yourself, "There is no way I could eat all of this stuff, so I'm not even going to try," and then close the lid and walk away hungry? Of course not.

Would you start with the sandwiches and eat one of each kind, move to the chips and have a handful out of every bag, and then take a bite out of every snack and a gulp from every drink? I hope not.

You would probably look at the sandwiches and find one that looks appetizing to you. Then you would grab a bag of Cheetos, maybe a couple of Red Vines, and a Diet Dr. Pepper, perhaps. Or you may choose to eat half of a sandwich and forgo the chips and sweets altogether in exchange for an apple and some celery sticks with low-fat Ranch dressing and a bottle of water.

Should you feel guilty for not eating everything in the picnic basket? Absolutely not. Then for goodness' sake, don't get overwhelmed by the number of ideas in the Rest Stops and give up before you even begin. It was never my intention that you try even half of the ideas in this book. I will be thrilled if you even implement one or two ideas—and you should be too!

May I offer a suggestion? Ask the Lord, as you read through this book, to place a specific anticipation in your heart about the area He wants you to focus on first. It would be my guess that if you aren't already nourishing your spirit daily, He is probably eager to spend some more time with you, and He may help you become excited about one of the ideas in one of the "Taking Care of Your Spirit" Rest Stops.

Notice I said *one* of the ideas in one of the Rest Stops. Don't try to tackle every area at once. You'll defeat the purpose. Remember, this book is about curing mom burnout, not adding more fuel to the fire. After that particular Rest Stop idea becomes a habit, you may want to look in the "Finding Time for Yourself" chapters to see if you can carve out a bit of extra time or choose an idea in the "Taking Care of Your Body" or other sections.

Let me assure you, I don't do all of the things I've included in the Rest Stops. I've tried many of them, some for longer than others. Some ideas I have tried knowing they worked well for others. But, I failed miserably with that idea, so I cut my losses and tried something else. Some areas come more naturally to me than others; the same will be true of you. That's OK. None of us is going to be strong in every area. Don't feel guilty about that.

My desire is to give you as many ideas as I can come up with in hope that you will discover one or two that jump off the page and change your life forever. And as you take better care of your own life, your family's lives will improve too. Remember, your family's well-being depends on yours.

part 1

Taking Care of Your Spirit

Your Spirit

Breathe in God and Exhale His Spirit

$\mathcal{F}$rom the time my children entered the adolescent years, we have shared something we call "window time." When they were really little, we called it "high/lows." Every night when I put them to bed, I asked them to tell me their high of the day and their low. This little exercise somehow made it easier for them to articulate their feelings.

As my children have grown, this bedtime ritual has expanded to include more probing questions like, "Did anyone hurt your feelings today? Do you have anything you need to confess? Are you confused about anything?" This is our special time to talk about whatever is on their minds.

It is amazing that even my sixteen-year-old son, Tucker, still looks forward to our "window times" each night. Of course, they have changed a bit now that he is a teenager. Some days he saves up questions or hurts or funny jokes, knowing he can share them with me during "window time." But lately, we mostly listen to music together. You see, Tucker is an awesome musician like his daddy, and he lives and breathes music. Every once in a while, he'll sneak in a question or a hurt still, but usually he just wants to play me the latest guitar lick he's learned, song he's written, or some amazing new band he's discovered.

A few months ago, I woke up suddenly from a great night's sleep. (Moms of small children, take heart—they really do grow up and sleep in, or at least they get old enough to turn on cartoons and pour their own bowl of cereal.) As I turned over on my pillow to see if my husband, Steve, was up making coffee yet, I noticed strange music running through my head. As I focused on the tune, I heard even stranger lyrics: "She don't lie, she don't lie, she don't lie—cocaine!"

What?! What had I been dreaming? Then it hit me: Tucker had played a CD by Eric Clapton for me the night before, and this was a line from one of the songs. I remember hearing that particular line and talking to Tucker about it, but I don't remember memorizing it so I could sing myself to sleep (or awake) with it later.

By comparison, yesterday I spent the drive up to the bunkhouse where I write listening to the iPod my mother bought me for my birthday. I've created several playlists of music I can listen to, depending on the situation. I have a playlist of upbeat contemporary Christian music to listen to when I run on the treadmill. I also have a collection of classical music for when I don't want the distraction of words.

When I'm feeling especially dramatic, I listen to my list of instrumental movie soundtracks and picture my life moving in slow motion. I also have a bunch of sermon CDs and audio books that I hope to listen to someday. And, of course, Tucker has put his own playlist of music on my iPod. (And, yes, we did have another talk about lyrics and the principle of "garbage in, garbage out.")

My favorite playlist is my collection of worship songs and choruses. This is what I was listening to on the long drive up to my writing retreat. I arrived late; read a few chapters from the latest Ted Dekker book; put our dog, Donut, in her crate; and drifted off to sleep. This morning I woke up singing, "Oh, Holy Spirit, You're my comfort. Strengthen me, hold my head up high. As I stand upon Your truth, bringing glory unto You, and let the peace of God, let it reign."[5] What a great way to start the day.

As moms, it is critical that we "live and breathe" Jesus, because what we inhale is what we'll exhale. Proverbs 23:7 says that our outward actions are prompted by our inner thoughts: "For as he thinks in his heart, so is he" (NKJV).

I've found that most moms have an easier time giving than receiving. From the beginning of this book, I've attempted to convince you that it is very important for you to learn how to receive so you will have more to give. It is equally, if not more, important, to discern the right and healthy things to receive so we can give wisdom and life to our family.

Be intentionally aware of everything you allow to enter through your eyes, ears, and heart. What are you watching on television and movies? What are you reading? What kind of music are you listening to? Are you surrounded by friends that fill you up or tear you down? It isn't just about you. What you allow inside your heart and mind is what will inevitably be poured out on your family. What you receive is, most likely, what you will give.

So, what should we be receiving? Jesus told His disciples, "Receive the Holy Spirit" (John 20:22). In the next few chapters and Rest Stops, I will show you practical ways to fill up with the Spirit through praise, Bible study, meditation, prayer, and rest. We will learn to take care of ourselves by taking time to receive from God.

Our only hope for being good mommies is receiving the power of Jesus to parent through us. That is why we must breathe in Jesus all through the day so we may impart life to our families. One of the best ways I've found to accomplish this is through Scripture memorization.

"All Scripture is breathed out by God and profitable for teaching, for reproof, for correction, and for training in rightousness, that the man of God may be competent, equipped for every good work" (2 Timothy 3:16–17).

Let's pull over to the next Rest Stop and learn how we can have "God breath" all day long by memorizing scriptures from the Old and New "Testamints." (I know, I know. My children are rolling their eyes with you.)

Your Spirit—Rest Stop
Filling Up with the Word of Life

 Keep the Word in Sight

Index cards are useful tools for all kinds of organizational processes and very effective as Scripture reminders too. This is one of the simplest ways I have used to hide scriptures in my heart and a method that worked no matter what age my children were or what season of life I was navigating.

Always keep blank index cards in your Bibles, particularly the Bible you use for your daily devotions. When scriptures come to life off the page, you have the tool immediately available to capture that verse and what the Lord is speaking to your heart. You can then place the index card somewhere in the house where you will be reminded of the Lord's voice.

Currently, I keep cards with memory verses next to my computer screen. These days, the computer seems to be the center of all my activities! But at different times of my life, I have used a variety of locations where I could readily view God's Word several times during my busy days. It is amazing how, without even consciously trying, these verses become committed to memory. Try some of these favorite spots:

❖ Bedside table or wall

❖ Medicine cabinet or dressing mirror

❖ Car visor

❖ Refrigerator

❖ Purse/wallet

❖ Kitchen sink

❖ TV screen

❖ Exercise equipment

❖ Bookmarks

❖ Next to wall clock

 ## Scripture Primping

One of the biggest challenges for me has been *not* making Scripture memorization another thing on my already overloaded to-do list. I have tried, instead, to find ways to incorporate scriptures into my daily routine. One of my favorite ideas is "Scripture primping."

Write out scriptures that coordinate with your primping tasks, and stick them to the mirror where you put on your makeup each morning. Read aloud and meditate on those verses, and you'll discover that soon many of them are committed to memory. Here are a few ideas to get you started:

❖ *Foundation—1 Corinthians 3:11*
"For no one can lay any *foundation* other than the one already laid, which is Jesus Christ" (NIV; emphasis added).

❖ *Eyebrows—Mark 9:47*
"And if your eye causes you to sin, *pluck* it out. It is better for you to enter the kingdom of God with one eye than to have two eyes and be thrown into hell" (NIV; emphasis added).

❖ *Eye makeup—Proverbs 16:2*
"All the ways of a man are pure in his own *eyes*, but the LORD weighs the spirit" (emphasis added).

❖ *Mascara—Proverbs 17:10*
"A *rebuke* impresses a man of discernment more than a hundred lashes a fool" (NIV; emphasis added).

❖ *Finishing powder—James 1:4*
"Perseverance must *finish* its work so that you may be mature and complete, not lacking anything" (NIV; emphasis added).

❖ *Blush—Luke 6:29*
"To one who strikes you on the *cheek*, offer the other also" (emphasis added).

❖ *Lipstick—Proverbs 12:19*
"Truthful *lips* endure forever, but a lying tongue is but for a moment" (emphasis added).

You can take this idea and expand it for other routine things you do in your day. Getting dressed could include scriptures about feet (while putting on your socks and shoes), scriptures about keeping your mind focused on the Lord (while brushing your hair), more scriptures about our mouths and words (while brushing your teeth), and scriptures about ears (while putting on your earrings).

 ## Group Scriptures Together

You can purchase spiral-bound index cards at Wal-Mart or office supply stores. You could use them as "flip cards," placing individual verses on each card for a chapter you are trying to commit to memory. After you have achieved that goal, you can keep the cards as refreshers or as a record of what you have committed to memory.

❖ You can even color-coordinate your cards. Blue could be scriptures on peace, red could be scriptures on anger, and so on. When you are struggling in a particular area, you can grab all the ones from that color and allow God's Word to minister His truth.

❖ I've heard Beth Moore talk about using index cards for grouping together scriptures that speak to a particular season or difficulty in your life.

 ## Other Scripture Memorization Helps

❖ I have a friend who put up a chalkboard in her kitchen and wrote a scripture every week to learn with her kids. Every time they passed by, they read it. The whole family ended up memorizing it without even trying.

❖ Write out a memory verse and place it on the front of the fridge or just above the water dispenser. Every time you reach for an ice-cold drink, say the verse aloud and fill your spirit with the refreshing living water from Jesus.

❖ There are also two resources I would highly recommend for Scripture memorization. The first one, MemLok, is a program that uses pictures as association points for the first word of a verse. Their Web site is www.memlok.com.

❖ The second program is AWANA Clubs. I have learned more scriptures than ever before by helping my kids with the weekly memory verses that are a part of this interdenominational kids' club. Check them out at www.AWANA.org.

I hope you realize that as much as I believe in the power of memorizing scripture, I also understand the season of life you are in as a mother. Sometimes, even the good things we know to do—and want to do—feel like one more thing on our to-do list. That is why many of the ideas in this Rest Stop have been ways to incorporate scripture in our lives without intentionally memorizing it. Thankfully, every time we even read the Word, aloud whenever possible, we automatically hide another nugget in our hearts.

Prayer is another wonderful opportunity to connect our hearts with the Lord in the middle of our very busy days. I discovered the privilege of personal communication with my Abba Father during my teenage years on *The Facts of Life.* As I share my story, I pray you will become even more excited about the prospects of an intimate, practical relationship with the Lord as you stick close to Him all day long.

2

Prayer

Keep in Touch with the Father

hile I was on *The Facts of Life*, "Blair" gained a lot of weight. (I'm going to blame it on her, since she was the one bursting out of her school uniform, not me.) In my autobiography, I write in length about how I learned to fill up with Jesus rather than attempting to fill my emptiness with food, so I'll spare you the details here.[6]

To make a long story short, one of the key turning points for me was the way I approached prayer. Up until that point, my prayer life closely resembled a trip to the department store at Christmas time to sit on Santa's knee. "Dear God, I need this and that, and please bless him and her, and thank You for all these gifts. Amen."

Not that God doesn't want to hear and answer our needs and bless our loved ones and give us gifts, but that is such a tiny sliver of the relationship He longs to have with us. He offers us friendship and guidance and revelation and peace and so much more. I determined that I was not going to pray to the giant Saint Nick in the sky anymore. I was going to enter into fellowship with the almighty God.

Now, what I'm about to write may sound a bit sacrilegious, and I sincerely don't want to offend anyone. But this really did help me and, hopefully, it may help some of you. I started by deciding not to close my eyes when I prayed. At the same time, I ruled out bowing my head or looking up to the heavens. At this point in my life, the way I wanted to approach prayer was more like a conversation than a spiritual discipline that I needed to do every day so I could check it off my "good little Christian" list.

With that in mind, I got up every morning, walked down the hall to the bathroom (which is where I had my daily devotions), sat down on the toilet (the lid was down!), and imagined that Jesus was sitting right across from me . . . on the rim of the bathtub. (I guess we should have traded places, considering I was sitting on the throne, but I didn't think about that at the time.) From this point of view I could look straight into Jesus' eyes and pour my heart out to Him.

We talked about everything from my guilt over gaining so much weight, to the loneliness I felt with my family so far away in Texas, to the really cute boy I had my eye on. (Remember, I was a teenager at the time.) This new perspective on prayer transformed my morning quiet time from religious routine to heart-to-heart conversations with my Abba Father.

As I cited in the Introduction, Jesus says, "Abide in me, and I in you. As the branch cannot bear fruit by itself, unless it abides in the vine, neither can you, unless you abide in me" (John 15:4). The bottom line is, we cannot be the mothers we want to be without the power of Jesus working in us and through us. If we want to see the fruit of the Spirit grow in our children's lives, then we must first make sure we are abiding in Jesus.

We don't use the word *abide* anymore. What does it mean? From the context, I figured it had something to do with staying connected with Jesus. But how, *specifically*, do we do that? Does it mean I need to read my Bible more? Go to church more? Pray more? Not necessarily.

When I looked up the word *abide* in my Bible software, I discovered that in the original language it had more to do with simply spending time with Jesus, hanging out with Him. Well, it didn't exactly say that in the Greek, but that was the basic idea. And what do people do when they hang out together? Well, obviously, lots of things—but the common denominator is *talk*! To get to know someone, to strengthen a relationship, to connect with each other, you talk. That is what prayer is: talking with God.

I know what you're thinking. *I don't have any time for my family, my home, myself, my responsibilities, and everything else as it is! How am I going to find more time to abide in Christ?* Trust me, our heavenly Father understands the seasons of a mother's life. There are times when a quick "I love You, Lord" first thing in the morning, followed by a "Protect my children," on the way to school, to a few random "Bless my husband," "Give me wisdom," "Help!" and "Forgive me" prayers throughout the day are all we can manage because we are so out of breath.

God understands. I understand. So does every other mother alive. Relax, pull over to the next Rest Stop, and take a breath as you discover a few, as "Blair" would put it, "brilliant ideas." I pray you find just the idea you need to enable you to carry on a conversation in prayer with your heavenly Father during this particular season of your life as a mother.

Prayer—Rest Stop
I Could Talk to God All Day

Pray During Everyday Tasks

I love using everyday tasks to remind me to pray for specific areas. This makes prayer more a part of my activities rather than something to feel guilty about if I don't get it done to my expectations.

When doing household chores, you can pray about specific issues in your life or your kids' lives or prayer needs within our community and nation. Here's what I mean:

Laundry Prayers

- While sorting—Ask the Lord to sort out your life, showing you areas that need to be reprioritized, changed, or thrown away.

- During spot removing—Pray to be cleansed from distinct stains and sins in your life.

- While adding bleach—Ask God to remove residues from things you encounter because you live in a fallen world.

- When pouring in the softener—Ask the Lord to soften your heart and give you a teachable spirit.

❖ When loading washer—Pray for people who need to be washed "white as snow" (Isaiah 1:18).

Folding Laundry Prayers

Pray for the person whose clothes you are folding. Here are a few examples to get you started:

❖ Husband's undershirts—Pray for integrity.

❖ Your nightgowns—Pray for unity in marriage.

❖ Son's pants—Pray for physical protection in all his roughhousing and tumbles.

❖ Daughter's shirts—Pray for modesty.

❖ Socks—Pray for God to be Lord of their lives from the top of their head to the soles of their feet.

❖ Panties and Briefs—Pray for purity, protection, and future reproductive health.

Prayers for Specific Areas of the House

As you clean, pray over specific rooms and related activities in those rooms:

❖ Family room—Pray for harmony between children, purity in TV watching.

❖ Kitchen—Pray for God to provide daily bread, healthy eating habits.

❖ Dining room—Pray for great communication among family members.

❖ Kids' bedrooms—Pray for peaceful sleep, time to relax, good study habits.

17

❖ Master bedroom—Pray for sweet sleep, for a healthy sexual relationship with your husband, for time to spend relaxing with each other.

Housecleaning Prayers

Pray about issues that correspond with your activity:

❖ Vacuuming—Ask the Lord to shine light on hidden areas to remove things you haven't even realized had become embedded in your life.

❖ Deep-cleaning bathroom—Ask the Lord to remove a problem area in your life or a family member's life.

❖ Furniture polishing—Ask the Lord to polish and refine areas in your life.

❖ Picking up toddler toys—Pray for patience to teach your children.

❖ Preparing meals—Pray for your hands to be God's hands in your children's lives; pray for provision.

 ## Quickie Prayer Times Can Add Up!

❖ *Pray in the car.* I know moms are rarely alone in the car, but when you are, turn off the radio and use that time to pray.

❖ *"Bookend" your days with prayer.* When you hop out of bed in the morning, kneel immediately and consecrate the day to the Lord. Pray by the bed at night and give thanks for the day.

❖ *Pray with your husband as you're falling asleep at night.* This may be the only time both of you slow down at the same time!

❖ *Pray on the way to church.* Pray out loud with your family for your church leadership each time you're headed to church.

❖ *Keep a blank monthly calendar in your medicine cabinet or in the kitchen.* As prayer requests come to you, jot them on specific days of the calendar, maybe over the next few weeks. Then, while getting ready or preparing a meal, you have a ready prayer list for that day. This is especially good for those people we tell we will pray for, but often forget, or the ones we want to pray for regularly.

❖ *Pray for our country's leaders.* Say a quick word of prayer for a national leader every time you see an American flag.

❖ *Pray on the way to school.* Have the kids pick an extended family member (especially those who need the Lord) each day on the way to school. Have everyone in the car say a one-sentence prayer for that person.

❖ *Pray for the lost.* Since my children were tiny, whenever we found a penny on the ground, we would pick it up and pray specifically for someone we knew to receive salvation.

❖ *Time to Pray.* A simple prayer reminder I learned many years ago from our pastor is to pray for your children, one by one, anytime you see a digital clock displaying the same number. For instance, when you see 1:11, 2:22, 3:33, and so on. It is amazing how many times the Lord has used this to prompt me to pray for my children.

Prayer Walks

❖ Prayer walks are a great way to get out of the house where you can see God's creation and afford the added benefits of exercise.

Many times, you also have privacy to pray out loud. Here are some ideas:

- Plan to walk early in the morning, before Dad leaves the house.

- After dinner, let the kids and/or Dad clean up while you walk and pray alone.

- Pray for your block or neighborhood. As you pass each house, pray for your neighbors. Even if you don't know their names or their needs, God can direct your prayers for them.

Pray the Scriptures

I've found several helpful ways to "pray the Scriptures."

If you have a friend in need of healing, find scriptures promising health and strength. Pray these verses, asking the Lord to make those promises true for your friend.

If your children are going through some particular issues, find scriptures that combat those areas of temptation or sin and pray for God's way in their lives as you read those words.

My Prayer Journal

For those of you familiar with my Web site (www.LisaWhelchel.com), in October 2004 I did a special project I originally called "The Pathway to Heaven Is Prayed with Good Intentions." You can find it on my archived journal entries under "Coffee Talk." But early in 2005, Howard Publishing did all of us a favor by putting it together in a book called *The Busy Mom's Guide to Prayer.*[7]

I love my prayer journal! In just ten minutes a day, twenty days a month, I can cover over one hundred prayer concerns for my family and world. It relieves my guilt and truly allows me to pray for all of the things I want to pray for. So you can either get step-by-step instructions for free from my Web site (look in the "Me in Mommy" section) or get the book. This prayer journal is a great way to organize and prioritize your prayer life. It's kind of an all-in-one prayer remedy for busy moms.

 ## A Week Without Prayer Makes One Weak

When you feel overwhelmed with prayer requests or concerns, perhaps you will find it helpful to categorize your prayer lists and divide them by the days of the week. For example:

❖ Monday you could pray for the sick.

❖ Tuesday could be the day you pray for widows and the needy.

❖ Wednesday is a good day to pray for your church and church leadership.

❖ Thursdays you could focus on America and social issues.

❖ Friday could be devoted to those in need of salvation—both known and unknown.

❖ Saturdays would be for extended family and close friends.

❖ Sunday would be designated for all the other prayer requests you've received that week.

Teaching Children to Pray

To teach our children how to pray, Steve and I tried to be creative with mealtime prayers. Rather than just "God is great, God is good . . ." when they were little, we'd ask them to finish sentences. Here are a few specific sentences we used:

❖ To teach them to always start with praise, we'd start with, "One thing I love about You, God, is . . ."

❖ To teach them to have grateful hearts, we'd use, "One thing I'm thankful for today is . . ."

❖ For learning to pray for others, "One thing I want to pray for some- one else is . . ."

❖ We allowed them to petition God for their desires (which increased dramatically around birthdays and Christmas!) by say- ing, "One thing I'd like to ask for is . . ."

❖ We made it a time to pray about character issues and relation- ships with one another with statements like, "One thing I'd like You to change inside me is . . ."

This was an easy method of teaching our kids what prayer is really about—it is a very personal and relevant conversation with God!

Prayer Partners

❖ Many online prayer bulletin boards exist. You can enter a pressing need and have thousands of people praying with you for that need. The following Internet sites are good places to begin:

22

www.dailyguideposts.com

www.family.org/prayerrequest

www.upperroom.org

❖ Many local churches also have prayer groups who communicate via the Internet and phone and who will agree with you for needs and concerns.

❖ There are a variety of prayer groups specifically designed for women and/or moms that you can be a part of. Moms in Touch is specifically designed for moms who want to pray for their children's schools (www.momsintouch.org). The World Prayer Center has online prayer meetings (www.worldprayerteam.org).

❖ Church prayer groups and Home Teams can be a huge blessing. When I was first in California, filming *The Facts of Life*, I was invited to Michael and Stormie Omartian's home group. Every week, a group of us in the TV/film industry would meet for prayer. The format was very simple: we'd each take an index card and write down each others' prayer requests as they were spoken around the circle. Then we would assign one day to each person in the circle. You prayed for the needs of the others in the group on your assigned day, and we all had the assurance that someone in the group was praying for our needs every day of the week. It was amazing to see how God answered our prayers!

❖ Another way to be accountable is to schedule a "prayer appointment" with someone each day or week. You can decide to call, meet, or e-mail and agree together for your prayer list and needs.

 **Prayer Luxuries**

You may not even be at a season of life where any of the following "prayer luxuries" are possibilities, but here are some ideas for you to tuck away for the appropriate time:

- ❖ Go away for a day and pray through a long list, spending quality time on each item and allowing the Lord to "talk back" to you.

- ❖ Spend time each day developing a prayer journal. Log what you are praying about and how the Lord is answering prayer. Take time to go back and review and see areas where He has changed your life or your kids' lives. The computer is great for this.

- ❖ Consider going on a prayer weekend retreat where you can be instructed and focus on talking to God, one on one. There are many organizations that offer prayer retreats, such as The Navigators (www.navigators.org) and Walk to Emmaus (http://www.upperroom.org/emmaus).

I used to read the apostle Paul's instruction to us in 1 Thessalonians 5:17 to "pray without ceasing" and feel like giving up before I even started. I could barely find time to pray first thing in the morning; how was I going to pray all the time? Something happened on the way to raising three children. I became so desperate for Him and His help in my life as a mom that I found myself praying all through the day about everything!

The same thing happened with my Bible study time. The emptier I felt, the more I hungered for God's Word. The more time I spent reading and studying my Bible, the more starving I became to be filled even more with the Bread of Life. Allow me to share with you the best "diet" I've ever been on, and I've tried them all!

3

Bible Study

Hungry for the Lord

What would you say to a friend who came up to you one day and shared, "I don't know what's wrong with me. I'm feeling weak every day; sometimes I can't even walk straight, and I find myself stumbling. I don't have the energy to live the life I know I'm supposed to live. I can't figure it out. I mean, I eat a big meal every Sunday afternoon at my mother-in-law's house, so that should be enough to get me through the week. Occasionally we have pizza on Wednesday evening, but we always have another huge dinner again on Sunday. Yet I'm still weak. I don't get it?"

You would probably look at her like she was crazy and explain, "You can't only eat one meal a week, or even two, and expect to be healthy. You have to eat every day!"

Yet you may have had this same conversation, even if only with yourself: "I don't know why I'm not living the abundant life I know God has for me. I'm not walking the straight and narrow like I should; instead, I find myself weak and stumbling. It doesn't make sense. We go to church every Sunday, sometimes even to special events during the week. Yet I still feel empty."

As I mentioned earlier, we were created body, soul, and spirit. Just like you have to feed your body every day to stay physically healthy, you also must feed your spirit every day to stay spiritually healthy. Jesus said, "I am the bread of life. . . . As the living Father sent me, and I live because of the Father, so whoever feeds on me, he also will live because of me" (John 6:48, 57).

You know it as well as I do—moms aren't allowed to get sick. If we do get sick, we are certainly not permitted to get in bed and sleep it off until we feel better. (Only babies and dads who act like babies have that luxury.) We must stay strong for everyone else. How much more important, then, is it for us to stay strong spiritually? You must take care of yourself and make sure you feed on Jesus every day.

I learned this truth at a young age. When I first became a Christian as a ten-year-old girl, I attended a little Baptist church down the road from my house. Each Sunday morning, I would insert my coins in the offering envelope and see how many little boxes I could check on the outside flap. *Gave an offering—check! Brought a friend—check! Read Bible daily—check!*

I'm very thankful I developed the habit of daily Bible reading early. Sadly, it wasn't until I was much older that I understood what King David meant when he said, "How sweet are your words to my taste, sweeter than honey to my mouth!" (Psalm 119:103). At first it was more like eating my vegetables. I knew it was good for me, but I can't say that I always enjoyed it. As I've grown, I can honestly say that I can't wait to get up every morning, grab my cup of coffee, and dig in to a delicious meal in the Word.

Join me at the next Rest Stop, and let's discover some tips for making sure you eat—and enjoy—a healthy meal every day. (By the way, it is my personal opinion that if carbohydrates were so evil, then Jesus would not refer to Himself as the Bread of Life!)

Bible Study—Rest Stop
Your Word Is Like Honey

The Word says that if we lack anything, we should ask and the Lord who loves to give good gifts will supply (Matthew 7:11). If you struggle in the area of Bible reading, begin by asking the Lord to give you a hunger for studying His Word. Soon you will be agreeing with King David. And who can resist honey?

 Daily Bible Reading Tips

Here are some super-quick ideas to help you get in your daily Bible reading:

❖ Listen to Bible story tapes with your children.

❖ Read one chapter in proverbs and five psalms each day to get you through them in one month.

❖ Break up reading time throughout the day—first portion in the morning, part during naps, part while waiting in line to pick up the kids at school, part at bedtime.

❖ Pick up a used set of Bible tapes or CDs on eBay. Listen to the Scripture while exercising, in the car, on your daily work commute.

❖ Pocket New Testaments are great for your purse, the car glove box, or the diaper bag so you'll have the Word with you when you can catch a few moments.

❖ Keep an open Bible in the kitchen, bathroom, schoolroom, or near your computer. Catch verses throughout the day—little increments add up!

❖ Leave the house a few minutes early to pick up the kids from school. You will not only be first in the car pool line, but you will also have time to "snack" on the Word. Sign up to have a Bible reading e-mailed to you each day. Here are a few to get you started:

www.bibleverses.com

www.christnotes.org

www.gospelcom.net

❖ For working moms, use your break time or lunch for Bible reading or study.

❖ Take twenty minutes while Dad and the kids are cleaning up supper to "go to your prayer closet" and catch some time to read your daily devotions.

❖ Read the Scripture aloud. Hearing the Word has even more impact than reading alone.

❖ Go to "Our Daily Bread" (www.rbc.org/odb) or other great devotional Web sites for a daily Bible reading and application.

❖ Have a variety of devotions, newletters, and articles e-mailed to you periodically. To sign up for the ones that interest you, visit: www.crosswalk.com and click on "Newsletters."

❖ Purchase an age-appropriate Bible or Bible devotionals for your children and do your daily devotions together. VeggieTales has a new family devotional with short Bible study, application guide, and short, fun activities for families to do together.

 ## Bible Study Resources

To strengthen your Bible-reading muscles, consider some of the fantastic Bible studies available at your local bookstore. Here are some of my favorites:

❖ I love all of Beth Moore's Bible studies! My favorite one is *A Heart Like His*, on the life of David, but a close second is about the tabernacle, called *A Woman's Heart: God's Dwelling Place*.[8]

❖ Kay Arthur has a whole series of inductive Bible study resources that can take you deep into the Scriptures.

❖ LifeWay has a great series of Bible studies. Some of the ones I've personally done include studies by Priscilla Shirer, Mary Kassian, Henry Blackaby, and T. W. Hunt. Each one of them took me to a new dimension in the Word.

❖ I was honored to be asked to write a Bible study for LifeWay as a companion to my book, *Creative Correction*.[9] This is an excellent study for moms who want more biblical knowledge and basis for disciplining children.[10]

Many of these Bible studies are offered weekly at local churches. Most churches provide children's programs during adult Bible studies, so your kids can learn about the Bible while you do!

For super quick "bites" of the Word, along with a mini-devotional, check out "DriveTime Devotions for Moms," a CD I recorded to help busy moms (and their kids) get a bit of the Bible into their hearts while driving to school.

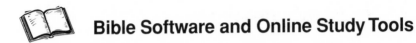 ## Bible Software and Online Study Tools

There are a variety of computer-related tools and ideas for strengthening your Bible-reading habits and study capabilities:

❖ Logos software (www.logos.com) is a great tool. I not only use it for book research, but I love to use it in my daily devotions and Bible reading.

❖ There are several Internet resources available. Bible Gateway is probably one of the best known—it offers a variety of translations for reflective and insightful Bible reading (www.biblegateway.com).

 ## Vary Your Bible Versions

Sometimes, reading a different version of the Bible will help you see the Scripture in a whole new way! Here are a few suggestions to spice up your Bible reading:

❖ Read one chapter a day in two or more different translations, such as English Standard Version, Amplified, New Living Translation, and so on. I don't know if it is the different flavors or the fact that I'm reading the same chapter multiple times, but I always get something unique from each translation.

❖ Read the Bible as a novel from paraphrased versions. These are not literal translations, but they can be very refreshing and insightful. These include The Living Bible, *The Message*, and the International Children's Bible. There is a place for deep Word study, and there is also a time for digesting the Bible in big chunks, grasping the big picture.

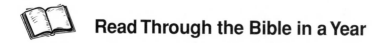

Read Through the Bible in a Year

You can pick up "through the Bible in a year" plans from many churches and online, both at the beginning of the year and throughout. Reading through the Bible is a great resolution to make each year, but don't become frustrated if you start on this plan and can't keep up the pace. Many times, we get discouraged or feel that we have failed, so we don't read the Word at all.

Remember, every word of the Word you put in counts! When I'm doing this plan, I end up taking at least two years to read through the Bible. As a matter of fact, I bought each of my children a "Through the Bible in Two Years" Bible. The readings are just the right length for a busy youngster (or busy mom.)

Any Scripture you get into your life *will* make a difference, so don't "grow weary of doing good" (Galatians 6:9)—try to get some Scripture into your life every day.

At this point in the book, I hope you are not already thinking, *How am I going to do all of this when I can't even seem to accomplish the things that are on my plate already?* Remember, just pick one area and one idea from that Rest Stop to work on. Don't attempt to tackle everything at once. As you implement one habit into your life, it will become a part of you and your daily routine, and you can turn your attention toward growing in another area without feeling overwhelmed.

Speaking of overwhelmed, I learned firsthand about the power of praise in a season of life when I was most completely weighed down with doubt, hopelessness, and exhaustion. If you can identify with any of these emotions, you will definitely want to read the next chapter.

4

Praise

I Was Called to Say I Love You

I remember one specific Sunday morning more than a dozen years ago. I was sitting on the front row of our church because my husband, Steve, played the organ. We were going through a hellish time in our marriage, and I was only sticking around for the sake of the children and my heavenly Father.

I'm naturally, by temperament, an extremely positive person. As a matter of fact, the glass is rarely half full to me. It is actually overflowing so much that it merely had to be poured into a taller glass so it may appear half empty. This particular time of my life is the one and only time I ever remember feeling hopeless. I simply could not see how the rest of my life was going to be anything but stuck in a bad marriage, with a husband who was unwilling to change, with no way of escape.

At the end of the pastor's message, we began singing a song we had sung as a congregation numerous times before. This time it was different. This time I desperately meant it. I stood to my feet, and, with my hands unabashedly reaching up and out to be picked up by my Daddy and tears running down my face, I sang:

Who can satisfy my soul like You, Jesus?
Who on earth can comfort me
And love me like You do?
Who could ever be more faithful and true?
I will trust in You,
I will trust in You my God [11]

For a few minutes, I caught a glimpse of hope, and I held on for dear life. If I had not fastened my gaze on what I knew was true of the character of God, rather than focus on the bleak future in front of me, I don't know how I would have survived those desolate years. Every word in that song is true, but I had to sing it in faith before I could sing it in celebration for the blessed redemption He eventually brought to our marriage.

I used to think worship and praise was about God. I wouldn't have said this out loud, but I thought it was something He needed—or maybe not needed, but at least wanted. I realize now that, in some ways, praise is really all about me. That sounds as heretical as my previous observation, doesn't it?

All I know is, whenever I sing about the Lord's awesome power, His faithful goodness, unquestionable sovereignty, and love without measure, I don't think I'm telling Him anything new, but I am often reminding myself of something I've temporarily lost sight of.

King David, for one, knew how to stir up his soul by remembering the many reasons God is worthy of our praise! I don't think praise can be articulated any better than he says it in 1 Chronicles 29:10–13:

. . . O LORD, the God of our ancestor Israel, may you be praised forever and ever! Yours, O LORD, is the greatness, the power, the glory, the victory, and the majesty. Everything in the heavens and on earth is yours, O LORD, and this is your kingdom. We adore you as the one who is over all things. Riches and honor come from you alone, for you rule over everything. Power and might are in your hand, and it is at your discretion that people are made great and given strength. O our God, we thank you and praise your glorious name! (NLT)

That sure puts our circumstances in perspective, doesn't it? That is one of the blessings we receive when we offer praise to God. When we remember His awesomeness, our challenges look smaller in comparison to His greatness.

Praise is often the last thing we feel like doing when we need it most. Maybe that is why it is often referred to as a "sacrifice." Hebrews 13:15 says, "With Jesus' help, let us continually offer our sacrifice of praise to God by proclaiming the glory of his name" (NLT).

Let me encourage you to *make* yourself praise the Lord. I know that sounds awful, but if you are anything like me, then you know what I'm talking about. Whether it is because we are too busy, or because we like to *do* something about our problems, or because we don't think we have a very good singing voice, or we weren't raised to praise the Lord out loud, or any other excuse, we have to get over it and discipline ourselves to proclaim the glory of God's name! It is worth it, because He is worthy.

Praise isn't optional—something we can treat as a "luxury" to "pamper" God or ourselves with once in a while "when we have time." Worship (like prayer) is powerful in spiritual warfare; it's a necessary and vital part of protecting ourselves and our children from the enemy. Praise has great power in fighting spiritual battles.

When you or your children are struggling with a particular issue or area, or when your household is struggling with an area, begin speaking praise over it. "Lord, I thank You that, in Your Word, You declare that You will supply all our needs according to your riches in glory. I thank You, Lord, for Your provision over this household. I praise You for favor in our jobs and for wisdom in learning how to be more frugal. Lord, You are the source of everything—I praise You for being our source today."

And if that weren't enough, praise feels good! Acts 3:20 says, "That times of refreshing may come from the presence of the Lord." God inhabits the praises of His people (Psalm 22:3). When we praise the Lord, He fills us with His presence and refreshes and refuels our spirits.

Whether it is out of the overflow of your heart or the aching emptiness of it, praise is the answer. Whether the words are directed as praise to God or reminders to yourself, worship is worthy.

Join me at the next Rest Stop, and let's discover fresh ways to remember God's "Godness" all through the day.

Praise—Rest Stop
Can I Just Tell You You're Amazing

♪

♪ Fill Your Days with Worship

Like so many other things we want to do, we have to find time to incorporate worship into our daily lives or it simply does not get done. Here are some of my favorite ways of pouring worship into our crowded days:

- ❖ Post in strategic places (refrigerator, car rear-view mirror, bathroom mirror) scriptures that express worship to the Lord or cause you to remember to praise Him.

- ❖ Keep a hymnal with your other reading materials. Before you curl up with a book or magazine, open the hymnal. If you don't know the melodies, just read them out loud as praise and worship.

- ❖ Admit it, you sing in the shower, so use that time to praise the Lord at the top of your lungs!

- ❖ Sing Bible songs in the car with the kids. We love Steve Green's *Hide 'em in Your Heart* CDs, which are Bible verses set to music. I also recommend *Seeds* Scripture CDs, Integrity's *iWorship for Kids* CD/DVD and *The Memory Bible* CD which also comes with a book. Keep these in the car, and listen to them often.

❖ Decide that for one day, whenever you begin talking to God either verbally or in your heart, you're not going to ask for anything or express any concerns. Instead, you are just going to give Him worship and praise.

❖ Use your exercise time to praise the Lord. My time on the treadmill often finds me praising or singing.

❖ Keep worship music playing around the house. The influence of good music in your house versus negative music or noise can be dramatic, especially for teens. Determine that your house will be a house of praise.

❖ Use mealtime prayers as learning times for teaching praise and worship. Sing your prayer or favorite worship chorus before the prayer. Use traditional songs, like the Doxology, for special occasions and holidays—to express thanksgiving and praise.

❖ Set an alarm or timer to go off every few hours. When it sounds, praise the Lord for five minutes. Kids, especially, will love this because they get to stop midstream with whatever they are doing and shout, sing, and praise the Lord. Or use it as a cue to crank up your favorite worship song and dance. Dad will be surprised, not knowing it's "worship day," when he comes home and the alarm goes off!

❖ Read a book on worship. Pastor Jack Hayford has several outstanding books about worship (www.livingway.org), as do many others.

❖ Strap on a CD player, pop in some praise songs, and sing to the Lord as you are vacuuming, dusting, or doing laundry or any of those other mind-numbing tasks.

♪ **Worship God for Who He Is**

Use the attributes of God (list as many as you can think of or ask your pastor) or your church's tenets of faith (usually found on their Web site or in their doctrinal statement) to express worship for specific things and issues you are dealing with.

For instance, your belief statement would include that Jesus is our Redeemer, the Holy Spirit is our Comforter, and so on. Use those characteristics of God to express worship about personal life issues. "Jesus, I'm so thankful You are redeeming my life from this particular area of sin. Thank You for the redeeming work You did on the cross, which enables me to put aside this sin and embrace Your wholeness for me." Or verbalizing praise like, "Holy Spirit, I am so glad You are the great Comforter and that You comfort my heart, helping me not to worry about . . ."

These lists of things describing God and His works for us can also be read aloud as prompts for praising the Lord—not for things or blessings, but for *who He is.*

♪ **Dance Before the Lord**

Let them praise his name with dancing.
Psalm 149:3

I love a story Beth Moore shares in her Bible study on the life of John. She tells about the first time she discovered the joy of dancing before the Lord. Her experience reminded me of when I was a little girl and how much I, like all little girls, loved to twirl around, flitting and floating like a ballerina.

We are God's special little girls, no matter how old we are. Our Daddy

God delights to see us dancing in His presence—joyous about Him and relishing our relationship with Him, which encompasses all of His provision, blessings, and covering of our lives. That truly is something to praise Him about!

So I decided to go for it—create my own ballet dance just for my heavenly Father. I'm sure it was nothing to look at, but it wasn't for anyone else to see. It was purely between my Daddy and me, from my heart to His. It was an awesome awakening in my spirit to the power of worship. Mind you, I was very sore the next day—my middle-aged muscles were asking, "What were you thinking?" But it was worth it!

Become a little girl again in your heart—dance and twirl and show your heavenly Daddy how much you delight in Him and how thankful you are for His care and love.

Do a Bible search (www.biblegateway.com) to find other new ways of expressing physical worship to the Lord:

* Clap

* Bow

* Kneel

* Lift hands

* Use musical instruments

♪ Don't Neglect Corporate Worship

I also believe it is critical for our well-being and our family's well-being to find a place where we are comfortable worshiping corporately. Find a good church. Attend regularly. Corporate worship is scriptural—"Let us consider how we may spur one another on toward love and good deeds. Let us not give up meeting together, as some are in the habit of doing, but let us encourage one another—and all the more as you see the Day approaching" (Hebrews 10:24–25 NIV)—and it brings all kinds of strength and encouragement to our lives.

Don't just attend a local church—get involved! Your participation is vital and will enrich the rest of the congregation. God calls us to worship Him both individually *and* corporately. One can become unbalanced without the other. So don't neglect this very important aspect of worshiping the Lord.

Throughout the Old Testament, sacrifices offered to the Lord are associated with a sweet aroma that reaches up to the Lord and brings peace. Many things are encouraging to me about this fact. First, that God considers my offering of praise to Him as "sweet." Secondly, the term "aroma' reminds me that with even a little squirt of perfumed praise, my worship can permeate the whole day. Lastly, wherever there is turmoil, division, unbelief, or anything else that threatens to separate me from trusting the Lord, all I have to do is muster enough faith to remember the faithfulness and goodness of God, and He will bring rest and peace in the middle of my storm.

I never thought about it until writing this paragraph, but Jesus was resting in the middle of the storm on the Sea of Galilee. When the disciples called on Him, He brought peace to the waves rocking their boat. Afterwards He turned to them and said, "Why are you so afraid? Have you still no faith?" (Mark 4:40).

When we have faith, and trust God completely, we can rest in the middle of the waves of doubt rocking our world. Resting requires faith. Hebrews 3:19 tells us, "We see they were not allowed to enter and have God's rest, because they did not believe" (NCV). Just a few verses down, Hebrews 4:4, 10 reads, "In the Scriptures he talked about the seventh day of the week: 'And on the seventh day God rested from all his works.'. . . Anyone who enters God's rest will rest from his work as God did" (NCV).

In the next chapter, we'll explore ways to show God we trust Him by obeying His command to rest. Obeying God in this area has been a tough one for me, but I'm learning. I hope you'll learn with me.

5

Keeping the Sabbath

God Will Take Care of Everything

I'm one of those people who likes to work, and I find it extremely difficult to relax. Being productive to me is fun; I get an adrenaline rush as I'm completing a project. So the Sabbath commandment is tough for me.

On top of all that, like most moms, I have way more things to do than I have time to do them all. It is very hard for me to justify giving up a whole day without accomplishing something. Of course, I understand that is the wrong mind-set. I know that, ultimately, nothing I could ever accomplish could be more important than honoring God; but when I'm being most honest, that is how I feel. And I know that renewing my relationship with God is the most important thing I could do, but it just doesn't feel *productive* enough to me sometimes.

My husband is an even worse workaholic than I am. (Strange, how none of our children appears to have inherited this particular trait.) One Sunday morning, Steve woke up and headed straight for the office in our home. As he sat down to his computer, he discovered a tiny yellow Post-it note stuck to the monitor. It read, "Don't turn on the computer on Sundays—God." The handwriting was suspiciously adolescent, but I guess that if God wrote the note with His fingertip, His writing could be a bit scribbly. (Who knew sticky notes were the modern-day stone tablets?)

I understand that as New Testament Christians living under grace, we are no longer required to keep the Sabbath. At the same time, "'All things are lawful,' but not all things are helpful" (1 Corinthians 10:23). I happen to think that the Lord commanded the Sabbath for our own good, so why would we want to be like the world and work ourselves to death?

I think it is ironic that, as a whole, we still consider nine out of the Ten Commandments to be valid for today. We agree that we shouldn't lie, steal, commit adultery, and so on. But "Remember the Sabbath day, to keep it holy"? Nah, that's old-fashioned, we think.

Or we may even think, *I can't just sit around and relax all day. That would be selfish!* Not only is it not selfish, but taking some time to rest and be refreshed is a provision directly from God's hands as a gift to us.

While doing research for this book I received the following "tip" via e-mail, and I was so touched I wanted to print it exactly as I received it:

Believe it or not my burnout stemmed from the fact I did not have enough time with my kids. I did not want time away. I wanted time to read to my 4 yr old and hear about their friends and watch a good tearjerker with my teen. The last straw was when my 11 yr old said she did not ever want to be a mom...it was no fun and they had to do all the work. When I relayed this story to a dear friend she stored it in her head and the following Wednesday she showed up at my house with dinner and dessert all made, a movie and some books for me to read to my 4 yr old. It was the most awesome evening I could remember in a long time. Sometimes our burnout is not because we are moms but because with all the other things...taxi, cook, teacher, janitor, maid, nurse we lose our chance to be moms. And isn't that why we got ourselves in this situation in the first place? Yes those chores are a big part of being a mom but there is something even more important. That primal need to be close to our children and cuddle. That is the best rejuvenator there is.

Isn't it wonderful that God, our best friend, has already arranged for us to have at least one whole day a week when we can "quit" our other jobs and enjoy the one we love most—being a mommy. To keep up the same frantic pace you do the rest of the week is not just a poor personal choice; it's disobeying God, and rejecting His thoughtful gift.

What's even more amazing is the observation that this particular commandment is the only one God chooses to illustrate with a personal example. "For in six days the LORD made heaven and earth, the sea, and all that is in them, and rested the seventh day" (Exodus 20:11). Are we really saying, "God may need to take a break, but I don't?"

Of course, we need to take a break. I'm all for working hard, being responsible, and being the best mommy possible. I think taking care of everything and everyone is simply in a mom's DNA. Being diligent is not usually the problem. God knew it would take nothing short of a command and a personal example to convince us to slow down long enough to take a *still picture* of our family and reflect, "It is good!"

Remember, rest is a key element in God's plan for all of us—never forget, even God rested! When we get physically weary, our exhaustion opens the doors for the enemy in so many ways: irritability, lack of focus, getting lazy in all of our other habits, and putting our emotions constantly on edge.

Think of getting adequate rest as the foundation. Without it, everything else falls apart. Proper rest is essential to everything else we are trying to accomplish, just like taking care of your health is essential to the health and well-being of your family.

God told His children, the nation of Israel, over and over again that by keeping the Sabbath, they were showing the other nations that they were different, they were set apart, they trusted God for everything. We long to be witnesses for the world. Could we start by saying no to shopping, tournaments, and overtime on Sundays? Let's show our kids, and the world, that the Lord's Day is special.

I remember as a little girl growing up in Texas that we had "blue laws" requiring everything, except drugstores, to be closed on Sundays. These days, Sunday is just like any other day of the week. How sad. I think we've lost something as a culture, and definitely as a family, by not setting aside the Sabbath. It is time for Christians to rise up and reclaim the Sabbath.

For me, I'm discovering that keeping the Sabbath is really a matter of trust, kind of like the principle of tithing. Do I trust God enough to follow this command and believe that ultimately He will enable me to accomplish all the things He deems important enough to do? When I force myself to remember that I can't do everything in my own strength anyway (John 15:5) and remind myself that ultimately anything of lasting value is going to happen by God's grace and power (2 Corinthians 3:5), I can relax and take a day off. Now I love it! As a family we've created our own set of Sabbath traditions, and Sunday truly has become a day we all look forward to celebrating.

When the chaos and crowds of people became so overwhelming that Jesus and His disciples did not even have a chance to eat, Jesus said to them, "Come with me by yourselves to a quiet place and get some rest" (Mark 6:31 NIV).

Meet me in the next Rest Stop, and we'll see if we can find a quiet place to get some rest.

Keeping the Sabbath—Rest Stop
The Rest Is up to You

It's hard to get too much of a good thing. Allow me to share a few ideas for a "mini-Sabbath," a "semi-Sabbath," and a "Super Sabbath." Remember, these are all in addition to honoring the Lord's Day as a family.

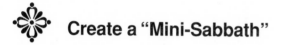 Create a "Mini-Sabbath"

Here are some ideas for creating your own "mini-retreat" during the week:

❖ Get in the car and pop in a worship CD or pray out loud, driving around for fifteen minutes.

❖ Have a spot, maybe in your bedroom, that is "your space." Keep your favorite things—such as potpourri, books, magazines, candles, Bible—within arm's reach. Retreat there on hectic days with a favorite beverage, even for a half hour, and spend some time nurturing yourself.

❖ Find a cozy spot to sit, eyes closed, and listen to your favorite music.

❖ Saturday mornings are a great getaway time for moms. Most of the time, Dad is home, cartoons are on, and you can sneak away for some relaxation. Or, have your husband take the kids to McDonald's for playtime without you.

❖ Require that everyone take a nap, regardless of age. Kids don't have to sleep, but they do have to read or play quietly in their rooms for at least an hour each day. This not only gives you some Sabbath time, but it teaches them to be independent and self-starters.

❖ Before Dad leaves for work, create a "code ring" in case he needs to reach you. Other than that, don't answer the phone for one day; just let it go to voicemail or to the answering machine. It's harder than you think! It may surprise you what a break you receive simply by spending an entire day without this one interruption.

Celebrate a Semi-Sabbath

❖ Coordinate with a good friend who has children the same ages as yours for a friendly mutual daycare service. Once a month, drop off the kids early in the morning. Having one day a month that is "yours" will feel like you won the lottery. Next time, your friend can drop her kids off at your house so she can enjoy a whole day to do whatever she wants.

❖ Take advantage of Mother's Day Out programs. Many churches have excellent programs for infants and toddlers that give moms a morning or two each week to have some time. Many offer either one day or two days a week. Many programs are able to arrange drop-ins as well. So, if you can't afford to enroll your kids in the program every week, you could drop off your kids for a day and spend it at home celebrating a "Mom's Day In." Don't answer the phone, don't do housework—just enjoy your day and your home. Take a nap!

❖ Go on a "date" with the Lord. Prepare a meal for your family, let Dad serve it, then you grab your Bible and journal and enjoy dinner at a restaurant. Spend the drive on the way there talking to the Lord. Ask for a table for one (although, you know there will actually be two in the party). Read, write, listen, and allow the Lord to speak "sweet nothings" into your heart about how much He loves you and cherishes you. Talk His ear off again on the way home.

❖ Anytime your church offers a women's event, do whatever you can to attend. They usually provide childcare, and as much trouble as it may be to pack up the kids and get out of the house, when it is over you are usually so glad you went.

✤ Set Aside a "Super Sabbath"

> *My beloved speaks and says to me: "Arise, my love,*
> *my beautiful one, and come away."*
> Song of Solomon 2:10

❖ Book a hotel room for yourself, and arrange for Dad, grandparents, or a close friend to keep the kids overnight. Go in January or September and spend that time praying through the upcoming year for your family. You can find some great deals on Priceline.com and many other travel Web sites.

❖ If you can't afford a hotel room, trade houses with a friend in a different city. Ask if you can "book" the room overnight. Offer her your house on the same night you stay at her house. Pack your Bible, a few good books, your comfiest pillow, and a journal to record whatever the Lord speaks to you during this time away with Him.

❖ Make it a point to attend weekend women's conferences whenever you can. There are so many good ones, including many great ones at local churches. Check out:

Hearts at Home	Paula White
Women of Faith	MomTime getaways
Extraordinary Women	Joyce Meyers
Women of Virtue	Kay Arthur
Living Proof Live	Anne Graham Lotz
LifeWay conferences	

and many, many more. You can find these retreats advertised in Christian magazines, on Web sites, and on TV. They can bring a great deal of strength and enrichment to your life.

❖ Send your kids to church summer camps, Vacation Bible School, and other children's programs offered at your church. These are not only great "Sabbaths" for your children, but you can use the time away to focus on spiritual things too.

❖ If you are a single mother who shares custody with your ex-husband, avoid the temptation to spend every weekend catching up on your to-do list. Put a "weekend retreat" on your calendar and spend some time refreshing your body, soul, and spirit.

Obviously, first and foremost, the Sabbath is a day set aside to rest from our work and honor God. In Leviticus 23:3, we read, "You may work for six days each week, but on the seventh day all work must come to a complete stop. It is the LORD's Sabbath day of complete rest, a holy day to assemble for worship. It must be observed wherever you live" (NLT). At the very least, do not forsake assembling together for worship. If you are not involved in a local body of believers, look around, visit a few churches near you. Make sure the Sabbath day begins by worshiping God together as a family with other "family" members.

Now, what was I going to write about in the next chapter? Oh yeah, the joy of journaling. One of the reasons I journal is because it helps me remember when I write things down, but I also love the thought that I can pass down the things I'm learning to my children—kind of like an eternal lecture, uh, I mean legacy.

6

Journaling

This Is My Story

They say the memory goes out with the placenta. I totally agree! I have a terrible memory. My short-term memory is great; that is probably why I never had any trouble memorizing my lines when I was on TV. It's the long-term memory that's the goner. (What was the name of that show I was on, again?)

I think this is one of the reasons I love scrapbooking so much. My children live such a blessed life, and I want them to be able to remember it (in case any of them inherited my memory, or lack thereof) so they can forever be thankful to the Father above, the Giver of all good gifts.

Scrapbooking is also an outlet for me to express love, respect, and encouragement for my family in a tangible way. Encouraging others comes naturally to me, so it is not as if my children aren't aware of how much I adore them. Still, I often see them pulling one of the scrapbooks off the shelf and finding the pages with their picture on it, where I have journaled about my hopes and prayers and reflections of them individually.

It is also a good thing that I have committed to journal once a week on my Web site. Most weeks, I get to the deadline for posting my "Coffee Talk" entry, and writing about my life is the last thing I have time to do because I'm so busy living it. Yet I'm always so glad I did it when I'm finished, not only because I receive such encouraging e-mails from other moms who find comfort in relating to my own challenges, but also because I know I'm leaving a treasure for my children to read someday. Wouldn't you love to know what your mother did and felt and struggled with when you were a kid?

Granted, there are many times I journal just to vent on the page rather than on my husband and children. I don't post these! However, I do feel a lot better afterward (or would that be after words?).

When my life feels most chaotic and overwhelming, it helps to take a moment while the kids are resting or playing quietly, (okay, maybe that would be more like a second than a moment) and focus long enough to write a quick paragraph in my journal.

There is something about seeing my thoughts on paper that provides clarity as I process the things I'm feeling and learning with the Lord. Even taking that quick moment and a brief paragraph to concentrate on myself helps me become a more centered mommy for my family.

I've found that the most important reason for journaling is to write down the things the Lord is saying to me and teaching me. Just like the funny things your kids say when they are little—you think you'll never, ever forget them, but you do. Sometimes you can't even remember which child said which cute thing. Luke 24:8 says that the disciples "remembered his [Jesus'] words." If you have an amazing memory, then perhaps this doesn't apply to you. But if you are like me, I need to write something down or I will surely forget it.

What a shame to forget something the almighty God, the Creator of the universe, said to you! The Lord tells us to "remember" more than two hundred times in the Bible, so remembering must be pretty important to Him. Tragically, I often forget things if I don't have a specific place, like a journal, to write them down.

As moms, we will often do things for our children before we will do them for ourselves. So if you won't take time to journal for yourself, then do it for your kids. One of the wonderful benefits of journaling is the blessing of passing our stories onto our own children so their faith can grow. Psalm 78:4 says, "We will not hide them from their children; we will tell the next generation the praiseworthy deeds of the LORD, his power, and the wonders he has done" (NIV).

In the next Rest Stop, we will talk about some ways to incorporate the blessing of journaling into our lives without making it a curse of one more thing to do.

Journaling—Rest Stop
Note to Self

I have learned there is a great deal of value to journaling. Maybe keeping a journal won't become as significant a part of your life as it has become in my journey, but I still think the practice of writing out your thoughts and experiences has a lot of merit. I have found many varied uses for this practice. But even if you find it a struggle, I encourage you to try some basic journaling—make a one-month commitment—and then evaluate its value to your growth and perspective.

 Getting Started

I think many of us "got our start in journaling" as a reflection and record of our daily devotional times. If you've never done any journaling, this is the best place to start.

Just get a blank notebook and begin recording anything the Lord speaks to you during your devotional times. Describe your feelings or what the Word meant to you—how it seemed to be speaking into your life or circumstance. Then write out your response to the Lord. It can be very simple. Something like, "Lord, I'm so glad You spoke to me about being more respectful of my husband's covering in my life. I want You to help me remember to put this in practice by not countering his correction of the kids and by recognizing his place as leader of our family life."

Take time once a week or once a month to review your record. You will be amazed at how much progress you see and how the Lord will use it to remind you of things He's spoken which still need to be carried out more fully in your life.

 ## Different Kinds of Journals

❖ Birthday Letter Journal—Every year, for each of my kids' birthdays, I write them a "birthday letter." I include all kinds of facts and figures about their accomplishments, their new interests, likes, dislikes, monumental moments, funny things they've done or said, and then record all the spiritual growth I've seen in them that year. These not only give my kids immediate affirmation and encouragement, but the letters become treasured memories to save for a lifetime. (As they've gotten older, I've also taken advantage of the opportunity to leave a lecturing legacy, as well, by including some of my motherly words of wisdom.)

❖ Gratitude Journal—Keep a journal next to your bed. When you wake up, write down five praises at the beginning of the day and five "thankfuls" at the end of each day. Use this as a tool for creating gratefulness in your heart when things are not running smoothly or when you are faced with a difficult circumstance.

❖ Cathartic Journal—Are you going through an exceptionally stressful season of life? Grab a journal and release some of that tension on paper by writing about your feelings and circumstances. The *Journal of the American Medical Association* (not a "journal" journal, like we've been talking about) reports that writing about stressful life events actually reduced symptoms of chronic illnesses in a clinical test. This simply proves what we instinctively know: journaling can help you deal positively with stress, which in turn, impacts health. Mental and emotional health go hand-in-hand with physical well-being. It must be that body, soul, and spirit thing we've been talking about.

❖ Marriage Journal—Use a journal to capture feelings for your spouse. Write down those moments when you have great admiration, pride, or love for your husband. Don't be afraid to record "PG-rated versions" of the passion you feel in your heart for him during special times of closeness. Record funny things that happened between you—your secret musings and private jokes. It is not only fun to look back on, but these can also spark new and renewed feelings of love when you are going through difficult times.

❖ Communication Journal—Do you sometimes feel like you and your husband are coming and going so fast that you barely have time to slow down and talk? Do either you or your husband have a more difficult time putting your thoughts and feelings into words? Do you crave deeper communication? Keep a journal on your dresser, or on the bar in the kitchen, or even in the "throne room." Take a few minutes, here or there, to jot down words of encouragement, or even difficult things you need to express but have trouble saying out loud.

❖ Prayer Journal—Keep a journal devoted to prayers—both your own creations as well as prayers you have read. If you've never read historical prayers, you should definitely read some books or do some online research. There is a great deal of doctrine and encouragement to be found there.

❖ Sermon Note Journal—Bring a journal to church and take notes as you listen to the pastor. The simple act of physically writing the notes guarantees you will internalize more of what was said. The fact that you can go back and redigest it means you can receive even more nourishment.

 Computer Journaling

❖ Cut and paste from a handful of e-mails you've sent and received throughout the day. This is an easy way to keep a journal or daily log of what your life looked like in this season of motherhood. Keeping a word processing document for this purpose is a great way to capture life events without formally journaling.

❖ Keep old calendars, digital and paper ones both. They may not officially be journals, per se, but they are an easy record to save and look through again years later.

❖ There are many journal software programs that make journaling fun and super-easy. Here are a couple I recommend:

The Journal www.davidrm.com

Life Journal www.lifejournal.com

❖ Create a file folder for each month and then a daily word processing document to record your thoughts. Save the file with the day's date. This is a very simple way to begin journaling.

❖ Send weekly e-mails to close friends and relatives describing the family's activities that week. Write e-mails to your mother-in-law so she can feel connected to your lives, even though you may live several states apart. She will love hearing about the kids' lives, and you will enjoy her responses. Save all the e-mails—they become a permanent record of your lives.

❖ Ever notice how entire books are published of nothing but a famous person's letters? Get a headstart on your memoirs by creating a file folder on your computer for saving your correspondence. You may think nobody would be interested, but I bet your family would beg to differ.

❖ Blogs, short for weblogs, are extremely popular these days. Basically, a blog is your journal online. It can be password protected and you have to "invite" friends to read it, but it is typically written to share with other people. Many families blog and post pictures to keep extended relatives and out-of-town friends up to date on the comings and goings of their lives. Blogging, is a relatively new, but fascinating option for journaling. I urge you to check it out for yourself and see if this alternative might be of interest to you.

www.blogger.com

www.sixapart.com/typepad/

www.livejournal.com

www.myspace.com

 MomTime Journal

One of my first endeavors as I began MomTime Ministries was to create the *MomTime Journal.*[12] But you don't have to have our printed version to create your own journal. Many women have said that they keep a separate book for each of these purposes. Others have written they keep a separate book for each child in the Forget-Me-Nots category I describe on page 63.

Open Heart

Sometimes you just need to pour out your heart to God. It may be when your heart is full of praise and overflowing. Then again, it may be when you are overwhelmed with grief or stress. Perhaps you are facing a difficult issue or a decision, and you simply need to talk it out. Create an Open Heart section in your journal as a place to get it all out on paper. Don't think about what you are writing; simply record what you are feeling. Fill these pages with unabashed worship, unfiltered emotion, and uncensored questions. Throw the doors to your heart wide open and invite Jesus in.

 ## Sweet "Everythings"

Have you ever experienced the thrill of a loved one whispering "sweet nothings" into your ear? Every once in a while, even when we're surrounded by children, we feel a chill that runs down our spine and recognize it as the breath of the Spirit speaking to us. And then, above the noise of a busy mom's life, we catch the voice of our heavenly Father whispering sweet "everythings" into our hearts. You may hear it during carpool, while listening to a preacher, during your Bible reading, or in the middle of the night. When you do, take out your prayer journal and write down that sweet "everything" before it turns into a sweet "nothing" again.

 ## Rhema Rays

Rhema is the Greek word used in the Bible to describe a single word or thought, as opposed to the entire Word of God. For me, it describes that moment when I'm reading my Bible and a certain verse or passage seems to jump off the page. It is as if the Lord shines a ray of light on a verse, even if I have read it a hundred times before, but suddenly I understand how it specifically applies to my life. I call these moments "Rhema Rays." Create a section in your prayer journal for you to stop—right then and there—and write down that scripture and what the Lord is saying through it to you at that moment.

 ## Thank-You Notes

I don't know about you, but my mother always made sure I wrote a thank-you note the moment I received a gift. Now that I'm a mom, I'm enforcing the same rule. It just makes sense; if someone took the time to give you a present, then they deserve a simple gesture of gratitude. Create a section in your prayer journal for you to write a quick thank-you note to the Lord as soon as possible after He grants you the gift of an answered prayer.

 ## Family Altars

In Bible times, the Israelites would often build altars to mark the place where they met God. The purpose of this pile of stones was so they would never forget what God had done. Each time they passed the altar, it would remind them to tell the story of their encounter with God to their children and grandchildren. This section is for you to write down your stories of when God meets you along the journey. It is amazing how time can erase or dim even the most unforgettable experiences. In your prayer journal, create a section to record your own "family altars" to ensure that you and your children will never forget the amazing ways God intersects your lives.

Forget-Me-Nots

How many times has your child said the cutest thing, and you've said to yourself, "I need to write that down before I forget it," but you keep putting it off, and eventually you forget it? My theory about why we don't take the time to record those priceless moments is simple—there just isn't a logical place to write them down. A common piece of paper is too easily lost, the "Baby Books" are usually stored somewhere up in the attic, and a computer somehow seems so sterile. The Forget-Me-Nots section is an essential part of your prayer journal, so that you will always have the perfect place on hand to take the time to immortalize the treasured words of your little ones.

As we wrap up this first section, "Taking Care of Your Spirit," I hope you are feeling refreshed already. My prayer is that these ideas will inspire a happy expectation that you really will be able to do something for yourself by connecting to Jesus and subsequently become a better wife and mother.

As important as it is to nourish our spirits, we also must feed and care for our bodies. Think about it. If your body lets you down (or you let your body down), then it will be much more difficult to take care of our families the way we desire.

Let's start with a little humor. After all, if you're like me, if you can't laugh about your body, you'll surely cry.

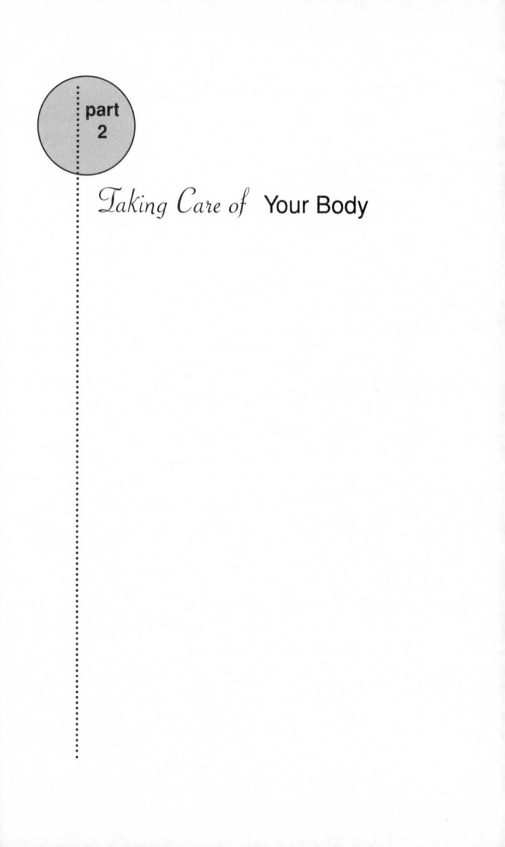

**part
2**

Taking Care of Your Body

7

Your Body

Temple Worship

*I*s it just me, or do you also find it odd that we can carry on a conversation about soccer and Little League and cutting teeth and the weather while our OB/GYN is in the middle of an examination? You would think we were simply chatting over a cup of tea. It's just plain weird!

Since we're on the subject (and since I'm assuming only women are reading this book), let's talk about mammograms. Obviously a man invented that horrid machine. I would like to invent a "manogram." You can use your imagination to figure out how it would work.

One of my favorite e-mails I ever received was from a friend the day before I went for my first mammogram. You've probably already seen it, but I get a laugh out of it every time:

> Many women are afraid of their first mammogram, but there is no need to worry. By taking a few minutes each day for a week preceding the exam and doing the following practice exercises, you will be totally prepared

for the test, and best of all, you can do these simple practice exercises right in your home.

EXERCISE 1: Open your refrigerator door and insert one breast between the door and the main box. Have one of your strongest friends slam the door shut as hard as possible and lean on the door for good measure. Hold that position for five seconds. Repeat again in case the first time wasn't effective enough.

EXERCISE 2: Visit your garage at 3:00 a.m. when the temperature of the cement floor is just perfect. Take off all your clothes and lie comfortably on the floor with one breast wedged under the rear tire of the car. Ask a friend to slowly back the car up until your breast is sufficiently flattened and chilled. Turn over and repeat for the other breast.

EXERCISE 3: Freeze two metal bookends overnight. Strip to the waist. Invite a stranger into the room. Press the bookends against one of your breasts. Smash the bookends together as hard as you can. Set an appointment with the stranger to meet next year and do it again.

You are now properly prepared.[13]

But we gotta do it! We must take care of ourselves, ladies. Remember, you have to take care of the "me" in Mommy—and that includes taking care of your body. If not for yourself, then do it for your family. If not for your family, then do it for the Lord. As 1 Corinthians 6:19–20 says, "You should know that your body is a temple for the Holy Spirit who is in you. You have received the Holy Spirit from God. So you do not belong to yourselves, because you were bought by God for a price. So honor God with your bodies" (NCV).

You may have heard that scripture a million times, but I want you to stop and read it again. Sometimes we get so familiar with verses that we no longer pay attention to what they are saying. Well, at least I do that. That is why I like to look up passages in many different translations. I used the New Century Version on this one. Doesn't it just spell it out for us? It is an act of worship to take care of God's temple.

We really don't have a choice about whether we have time to go to the doctor or the money to take vitamins, or whether we should go to bed at a decent hour instead of staying up to finish some work or if we should reach for a glass of water instead of another Diet Coke. If it is good for our body, then we must do it.

I think we've all heard tragic stories of moms who were so busy taking care of everyone else, they failed to take care of themselves until it was too late. Let's make sure we don't make that same mistake in the name of laying down our lives for others.

Jesus made the ultimate sacrifice of laying down His body to redeem ours. What a great way to say thank you by taking care of the gift He gave us.

Just this week, Steve went in for his first colonoscopy. I thanked him all the way to the doctor's office and back home. I felt so loved and cared for, knowing he was going through all of this for the children and me because he wanted to stick around and be with us for a long time. (When I told my mother the fact that colon cancer was the second-leading cancer killer, she remarked about her husband, "I better tell Roy to get his butt to the doctor!")

Here's another thought. I bet you love to make your house a homey place for your husband and children. Well, your body is the home of the Holy Spirit. Are there a few areas you might want to tidy up a bit? Keep in mind, it is harder to provide a healthy, happy home for our family when our "home" is in desperate need of repair and refreshing.

I'm not talking *Extreme Makeover: Home Edition*— just a few easy home renovation ideas that won't break your time budget. Pull over with me to the next Rest Stop, and let's start refurbishing.

Your Body—Rest Stop
Time for Some Body Work?

Rest Is Critical

One of the best ways we can take care of ourselves is by getting enough rest. Yet for moms, especially young moms, this can be challenging. And as you get older, they say insomnia increases. You can't win for losing sleep.

Here are some ideas for getting the rest you need:

❖ First, be realistic about how much sleep you need. Eight hours should be your goal. You may be able to survive on six or even less, but surviving is not the goal; thriving is.

❖ If you have short nights because of kids' illnesses, work, or other emergencies, try to spend extra hours sleeping other nights or on the weekend. Don't let yourself get too rundown and exhausted. Invest a few bucks in your health and hire a sitter to come watch the kids while you take a nap.

❖ Nap whenever small children are napping rather than trying to get things done. If you can't do this every day, pick a day or two a week when this is your pattern.

❖ Give yourself permission to let things go undone! If the choice is between cleaning the kitchen or going to bed and getting your eight hours of sleep, leave the kitchen for in the morning and sleep!

Vitamins Are Crucial

❖ I think vitamins are a second key to overall health and well-being. I know everyone has their favorite vitamins. We use Juice Plus (www.juiceplus.com). We also love a product called Total Recall (www.feedmybrain.com), which is specifically designed to enhance mind sharpness. It's great for school-age children who are constantly learning and expanding their minds, but Steve and I use it as well. There are also many Christian-based doctors and nutritionists who have brands available, complete with books on health and nutrition.

❖ You can also consider starting with a single "one-a-day" supplement and branch out from there. The drug aisles are filled with all kinds of special formulas.

❖ A good option for women, especially young women who are still menstruating, is a generic, over-the-counter prenatal vitamin. Several national drugstore chains have their own brands. They are an economical choice because they have extra calcium and iron, which is so important for women's health. And if you are still thinking about adding children to your family, they have the added benefit of giving you the daily requirement of folic acid, which is essential from the very first days of pregnancy.

Water Is Essential

Drinking adequate water—on average, eight to ten glasses per day—is also essential to nurturing our bodies. There's really no excuse not to keep yourself hydrated; after all, drinking water is not hard, costs nothing, and doesn't add anything to your to-do list. We all know this, but here are some ideas for getting enough water every day:

* Keep a cold pitcher of water (with lemon or lime, if you like) in the refrigerator. Reach for it instead of tea, soda, or juice.

* Keep individual water bottles handy to grab as you're running out the door. If budget is an issue, buy a large reusable water bottle, and add cold water as you're heading out the door. This is a great way to have ice-cold water for an extended time period.

* Make a decision to order only water with all meals eaten out, including drive-thru.

* Make popsicles out of water and lime or water and lemon juice. Grab one as a special treat instead of something else.

Physical Tune-Ups Are Vital

Having regular medical checkups is essential to keeping your body "in tune," just like a car or any other fuel-burning device!

* **Mammograms:** Have a mammogram every one to two years starting at age forty.

* **Pap Smears:** Have a Pap smear every one to three years if you have been sexually active or are older than twenty-one.

❖ **Cholesterol Checks:** Have your cholesterol checked regularly starting at age forty-five. If you smoke, have diabetes, or if heart disease runs in your family, start having your cholesterol checked at age twenty.

❖ **Blood Pressure:** Have your blood pressure checked at least every two years.

❖ **Colorectal Cancer Tests:** Have a test for colorectal cancer starting at age fifty. Your doctor can help you decide which test is right for you.

❖ **Diabetes Tests:** Have a test to screen for diabetes if you have high blood pressure or high cholesterol.

❖ **Depression:** If you've felt "down," sad, or hopeless, and have felt little interest or pleasure in doing things for two weeks straight, talk to your doctor about whether he or she can screen you for depression.

❖ **Osteoporosis Tests:** Have a bone density test at age sixty-five to screen for osteoporosis (thinning of the bones). If you are between the ages of sixty and sixty-four and weigh one-hundred-fifty-four pounds or less, talk to your doctor about whether you should be tested.

❖ **Teeth:** Don't neglect your teeth. Schedule a complete cleaning and checkup annually.

❖ **Eyes:** Is it time to have your vision tested again? Just today I had to change the font size on my computer screen from "12" to "14." I think I better take my own advice and see if I need to bite the bullet and check into some reading glasses.

Create a place where you keep record of these, and be sure to include your doctor's appointments in whatever organization or calendar system you use.

Remember, physically caring for yourself continually gets put at the bottom of the list, but your health is essential to your goal of being the wife and mother you want to be. So it is very important to make time to get these checkups done. Besides, think of all the fun time you'll get to spend reading magazines in the waiting room—that's a bonus benefit!

Throughout this book, I will consistently remind you to resist the temptation to feel more guilty while reading all the things you aren't doing. Remember, bite off a small chunk at a time; better yet, just nibble a bit. Now, here's where I contradict myself. If you are due for one of the tests that are recommended for a woman your age, I want you to stop right now and make an appointment. If money is an issue, make the appointment anyway. I will pray with you that God will miraculously provide for your need to care for His temple.

Lecture over! I'll trust that you either are all caught up on your exams or you have simply resumed your reading after a short phone break.

I think you are going to enjoy this next chapter. I couldn't decide whether to title it "Pampering" or "Beauty." I ultimately compromised by using both titles for the chapter and the Rest Stop. Do you remember that song, "I Enjoy Being a Girl?" Hum that tune while you read about some of the privileges of being uniquely female.

8

Beauty

The Beauty of the Lord Is upon Us

When I was a little girl, I was a bona fide tomboy. I loved to climb trees and hunt for crawdads, and my best friends were always boys. I only owned one dress, and the sole reason I had that one was because I had to wear it as the flower girl in my cousin's wedding. I was born a "full-figured" girl, so I could never squeeze my thighs into the cute jeans of my day, Dittos and Luv-its. That was OK; I preferred Wranglers cowboy jeans anyway.

I distinctly remember crying in the middle of a Payless Shoe Source because my mother would not allow me to buy the boys' platform shoes I had fallen in love with. I loved flannel shirts in the winter and T-shirts in the summer. My idea of shopping was leafing through the Sears and Roebucks catalog every fall, circling a new jacket and a couple of school outfits for my mom to order.

Comfort was (and still is) king in my book. Much to my children's chagrin, I have been wearing many of my favorite outfits since before they were born. I own one pair of black boots, black heels, black flats, black sandals, one black purse, and two pairs of white tennis shoes—one for casual and one for dressy. (Yes, I sometimes wear tennis shoes with dresses. Of course, I do put on my frilliest pair of socks.)

You probably think I'm joking about this, but just ask my friends or my family. I hate shopping and loathe trying on clothes. I feel fat in everything I put on, and I don't have any kind of knack for accessorizing. Instead, I have a half dozen easy outfits I wear all summer and another six or so comfortable outfits for the winter.

In addition, I have what my mother affectionately calls my "uniforms." I usually have two nice suits that I wear to every speaking engagement for a whole year. Then I buy two more for the next year. I also have two outfits for interviews and meetings. Oh, and I have one nice dress in case I'm speaking somewhere dressy. Each of these "uniforms" includes the jewelry and shoes. So it appears that I'm put together. Ha ha!

I'm about as opposite of "Blair Warner" as they come. Besides the fact that I'm not rich, I'm also not girlie at all. I keep one easy hairstyle for about a decade. I don't enjoy massages or facials. My nails never get long enough to make a tapping sound on the keyboard. I only wear makeup when I'm going out somewhere, and my idea of foundation is flesh-colored powder.

Secretly, I really admire women who have the gift of beauty. You know the ones I'm talking about—even if they are wearing jeans and a T-shirt, they look like they stepped off the screen from an allergy medication commercial. Their houses are filled with frames and trinkets that somehow look eclectic rather than cluttered. When they give a present, the wrapping is more beautiful than the actual gift.

My younger daughter, Clancy, is like this. She has a flair for putting together an outfit from Target and making it look like she grabbed it off of a mannequin at Nordstrom. She feels the same way about shoes as I do about books. Her room is yellow and turquoise and brown—and it looks fabulous. She has a lighted palm tree in one corner and a stack of hatboxes in the other, and I'm expecting the designers from *Trading Spaces* to pop out at any minute.

Yesterday, Clancy and my husband, Steve, brought home a vase of peach roses. Clancy announced that when she grew up, she was going to have fresh flowers all through her house. I could certainly appreciate the beauty of the flowers, but, for her, it went deeper. They filled up her senses, very similar to the way I see her react when she walks into a mall.

I think most women are more like Clancy than like me, but to whatever degree, we all appreciate beauty. My personal opinion is that it is part of being created in God's image. Genesis 1:27 says, "So God created people in his own image; God patterned them after himself; male and female he created them" (NLT). God is not half male and half female; it is more like He is 100 percent male and 100 percent female.

I believe we reflect God when we appreciate and exhibit beauty. Psalm 90:17 encourages us to "let the beauty of the LORD our God be upon us" (NKJV). God's glory is revealed in His creation, and enjoying that beauty is an act of worship.

What is the purpose of a gorgeous sunset? Is there a reason a genuine smile is so beautiful? Why is the smell of dawn so intoxicating? Can you tell me the rationale behind creating koala bears so cuddly? And what's up with clothing the lilies, after all? I'm sure there are probably natural and logical explanations for these questions. But let me ask you: could beauty for beauty itself be enough of an answer? I think so.

Even if you can't afford the time or money to be professionally pampered often, invest a little bit in yourself every day. Avoid the temptation to stay in your jammies until noon, only to change into a pair of sweats. Believe me, I know it is so much easier to grab a ponytail holder than to go to all the trouble of styling your hair, but take the extra fifteen minutes and do it anyway.

You'll feel so much more refreshed and beautiful. The kids may not notice how lovely you look, but your husband will be thrilled. You know he will!

At the very least, brush your teeth, spritz on some perfume, dab on a little lip gloss and throw on a pair of jeans before your husband gets home. Men are visual creatures. Thankfully, I think they also have questionable eyesight. When I feel my fattest, ugliest, and frumpiest, all I have to do is put forth the tiniest effort to beautify myself and my husband thinks I'm gorgeous. Trust me, your husband feels the same way. He will also think you are beautiful because the time you took to invest in yourself tells him that he is worth fixing up for. Your respect is more attractive to him than a flawless face or figure.

Now, let me ask you a question. If you are going to take that fifteen minutes at 4:45, then why not go ahead and take it at 8:45 instead? Do it for your husband—and yourself!

Remember, this fifteen minutes is the minimum you should try to invest. Every once in a while take thirty minutes and exfoliate, or use a deep conditioning product for your hair, or apply a facial mask. Don't forget to tweeze or wax your moustache, eyebrows, or billy goat chin hairs! I have to tell you a story about this one. I was teaching a kindergarten Sunday school class and had a little boy innocently crawl up into my lap and say, "You've got a moustache just like my daddy!"

So many times, even taking care of the things we really want to get done are put aside in the rush of raising our kids and managing our households. This jarred me to the reality that I needed to spend a little more time taking care of Lisa!

Hopefully, this chapter has convinced you to spend a little more time enjoying the privilege of being a woman of beauty. Pick one of the following Rest Stop suggestions and, for a few minutes, trade in the "Pampers" for some pampering.

Beauty—Rest Stop
From "Pampers" to Pampering

 Everyday Beauty

Here are some of my favorite "everyday" beauty tips that can be used just in the course of hectic life:

❖ Pick up a bouquet of flowers for yourself at the grocery store.

❖ Put on perfume—even if it's just you and the kids at the house for the day.

❖ Get fully dressed in the mornings—hair, makeup, matching outfit, shoes. This will make you feel special even on the most routine days.

❖ Serve yourself coffee or tea in your favorite china cup rather than the sturdy mug!

 Pamper Yourself!

Choose one night every month when Dad takes the kids out for a few hours and you have the house to yourself. Instead of doing something "productive," indulge in one of these:

❖ Take a bubble bath by candlelight. Pull out the ol' loofah, body scrubs, pumice stones, and anything else you can find hidden under the cabinet. Take an extra long time and treat your body to the deluxe wash.

❖ Invite girlfriends over and have your own monthly "spa night." Everyone can bring their supplies, and one month you can do each other's nails, then give pedicures, facials, makeup tips, etc. Everyone can bring their favorite products, and you can sample and try new things.

❖ At your next haircut, be adventurous and get a new hairstyle! Go ahead and take the plunge. I've been known to keep the same hairdo for a decade. I'm loosening up in my old age and trying all kinds of new styles. Some I love, some I hate, but, hey, it's only hair and it always grows back. Live a little. If you find you are wearing your hair in a ponytail most of the time because you just don't know what to do with your hair, that might be a good indication that it is time to visit a hair salon for some professional help.

❖ Go to the mall specifically to purchase new lingerie. Take time and find a bra that fits. You may want to get a sitter for this trip. Have you ever tried to buy a new bra with the kids in tow? Not a good plan! Try a new style of panties. Maybe even a thong for those pesky panty lines. (Although, those things look like "butt floss" to me.) While you're there, buy something special for nighttime wear (even if you only wear it for a few minutes). Think about it: Do you feel prettier in lace or flannel? Would you more likely be in the mood wearing a nightie or an oversized T-shirt? Splurge on something especially feminine. You won't be the only one who benefits from this indulgence.

Beauty on a Budget

If your family budget is tight, consider these low-cost variations:

❖ Short nails are in! If you don't have money to splurge on a professional manicure, pick up one of the "One-Minute Manicure" type
scrubs, rub some on your cuticles, trim your nails, throw a coat of
clear polish, and—voila!

❖ Find a local massage school in your area and enjoy a low-cost
massage!

❖ Beauty schools and colleges offer great budget-conscious
makeovers. Make sure the teacher is present and paying attention, and watch the student carefully—don't be afraid to stop her
and discuss it further. But especially for simpler procedures like
pedicures and manicures, this is a great option.

❖ Go to www.Marykay.com or www.arbonne.com and find a con-
sultant in your area. Be upfront—tell her that you and your friends
don't have lots of money but would enjoy a night when she could
come and make her presentation and do free facials. New con-
sultants need the practice, and most of them are very willing to do
this because they know most women spend something on cos-
metics at some point, so they are building their future customer
base. There are lots of other companies as well; just search the
Internet and network with friends to find new opportunities.

❖ Do some fancy footwork and give yourself a spa pedicure:

• Soak your feet in warm water with Epsom salt.

- Use a pumice stone or exfoliating scrub all over your feet, concentrating on the heels.

- Push back your cuticles.

- Clip your toenails straight across.

- Rinse feet and pat dry.

- Apply lotion liberally and massage feet.

- Wrap feet with plastic bags, Ziploc bags, or Saran Wrap for fifteen minutes. (For added effect, put slippers on to add extra warmth.)

- Paint toe nails in two thin layers.

- Add a top coat of clear nail polish.

- Give your toes plenty of time to dry before slipping on some sandals and showing off your beautiful feet.

 ## Indulgences

❖ Get a shoulder, neck, and hand massage. You can usually pay by the minute and feel remarkably refreshed for five or ten dollars.

❖ At least once a year, at the beginning of sandal weather, get a professional pedicure. Your toenails grow incredibly slow, so this is all you'll really need for the year. Splurge on the paraffin wax treatment—it is worth it!

❖ Budget for a facial. You *need* this, really. Tell your husband I said so. I'm the worst about this. If I'm not careful, I can go years without scheduling a facial, but it really is important to deep cleanse your pores regularly.

Make a "Pampering Wish List"

Most husbands appreciate your giving them suggestions for birthdays, anniversaries, Mother's Day, Christmas, etc. So why not choose one of those occasions as the time to give your beloved a list of special pampering and indulging ideas he can draw from? Give him very specific info: your favorite nail salon, your favorite hair colorist, your favorite brand of face mask, your favorite flavor of bubble bath, and so on. Tell him that, for the whole year, you want nothing practical or essential—you just want to be pampered!

Could I recommend a wonderful book on the subject of beauty? My friend, Angela Thomas, has written an incredible book entitled, *Do You Think I'm Beautiful: The Question Every Woman Asks.*

I realize I'm asking you to do one more thing, actually two more things: buy a book and then find time to read it. Trust me, I wouldn't suggest you add one more thing to your already very full life except I know that in the end you will have gained much more than you had to give up. Angela's message is especially timely as we head into the next chapter.

I hope you feel beautiful. If you don't, I understand. Remember, my name is Lisa, not Blair, and I struggled for years because of the value society places on outer beauty as the definition of beautiful. Allow me to share some of my story.

9

Healthy Eating

Send in the Clones

I do a lot of interviews these days as I'm promoting various books and speaking engagements. Inevitably, the radio talk-show host or newspaper reporter will sheepishly confess, "I had the biggest crush on you when you were on *The Facts of Life*." Often, at women's events, ladies will come up to me and giggle, "My husband was in love with you when he was a boy." I get this all the time, and it blows my mind.

Please don't think I'm fishing for compliments when I tell you that I was completely oblivious to this kind of attention when I was on the show. I had no idea that young men across America had crushes on me. I was so focused on the extra pounds I was carrying around that I couldn't see how anyone could think I was attractive. The confidence with which "Blair" carried herself was believable only because of the lines written for me to say, my love for acting, and the fun character I was privileged to play.

From my point of view (I was looking through a wide-angle lens), all I could see was the fact that I was letting the producers of the show and my fans down because I had gained so much weight.

I mean, how could I play the part of a girl who was in love with herself if I hated my own body? I felt like the whole world was making jokes about my getting fat. It didn't help that magazines and talk-show hosts often used my weight gain as comedy fodder. Ever hear the one about the girls from *The Fats of Life*?

A strange thing has happened in the last few years. The girls who grew up watching the show are now grown women, many of them moms who are my age. Regularly, a young, average-sized woman will approach me at the product table after a speaking event and tell me, "I used to love to watch you on television because I could relate to you since you were my size." Or they say, "I wish there were more roles on TV these days like the one you played. All of the actresses nowadays are pencil thin, and I worry about my daughters and potential eating disorders because of it." (By the way, that reminds me of a line from the show that "Natalie" said: "I'd rather be a happy magic marker than a skinny pencil any day!")

It is critical that we not base the standard for how we look on Hollywood's perception of what is beautiful. First of all, it is completely unrealistic. Who in the world has two to three hours a day to work out? And do you really think you could chase children around all day on a diet of grapefruit juice and alfalfa sprouts? It isn't possible, so don't beat yourself up about the fact that you don't look like a *Vogue* model. (*Vogue* models don't even really look like that!)

I remember a photo I had taken while on *The Facts of Life*. I was so worried because on the day of the photo session I woke up with a huge zit. I tried everything to cover it up, and of course, only made it worse. I was so naïve. When I arrived at the studio, the photographer acted like I was a country bumpkin for even giving it a second thought. "Don't you worry about a thing, darlin'. We'll take care of that later; nobody will ever have to know." When all was said and done, he not only airbrushed my pimple away, but he also shaved off a few pounds by "contouring" my chin and cheeks. Now that is my kind of diet!

Maybe that is why everyone starts looking alike in Hollywood. They must all use the same software program. How boring. If God's other works of art are any indication, He likes variety. Consider flowers, fish, animals, and trees. They come in all shapes and sizes. Every flower is not a lanky sunflower. We do not have a sea full of slender eels or a safari replete with graceful giraffes. Then why do we all want to be tall and skinny?

Look at the trees. Are they all lone pines? No, as a matter of fact, many of the most beautiful trees are the largest and oldest. Have you noticed that we measure a tree's age by the width of its trunk? Sound familiar? It is a fact of life (sorry) that our metabolism slows down as we get older. Unless we starve ourselves progressively more from year to year, we are going to gain weight as we get older! And unless we succumb to "the knife," we are going to get fatter and more wrinkled with age. Is this a flaw in the original design? Did God make a mistake?

Isaiah 44:24 says, "Thus says the LORD, your Redeemer, who formed you from the womb: 'I am the LORD, who made all things, who alone stretched out the heavens, who spread out the earth by myself.'" Just a few verses down the writer says, "Woe to him who strives with him who formed him, a pot among earthen pots! Does the clay say to him who forms it, 'What are you making?' or 'Your work has no handles'?" (Isaiah 45:9).

Perhaps you are saying to yourself (really it is to God, but you wouldn't dare actually say this to His face), "I don't want to have this body shape. I want to look like (fill in the blank). The problem isn't the lack of 'handles'; it is the presence of them! What was God thinking when He created me? Why couldn't He have made me thin and beautiful?"

Let me ask you a question: could you be content looking the way God created you? I really wrestle with that. There is a certain weight that no matter how hard I try I can't seem to get below. By Hollywood's estimation, I am about thirty pounds too fat. By a doctor's chart, I should lose at least ten pounds. In my blue jeans' opinion, I have about five pounds too much to easily get around. I'll probably always struggle with a few extra pounds, but as I get older I'm learning to be comfortable in my own skin, even if it weighs more and sags more than the clones in Hollyweird.

Healthy eating is one of the areas where I am "naturally challenged"—an issue that takes a great deal of focus and determination on my part to make good choices for myself and my family. Because of that, I have to approach it very practically and efficiently.

I also have to try to stay focused on eating healthily versus gravitating toward weight-loss-only goals. The two issues have always been tied together in my mind, which is probably the case for most of us. But I don't *always* want to be struggling with the emotional issues of weight loss, and I believe turning my mental focus toward healthy eating can help steer me in the right direction.

Healthy eating isn't just about losing weight. It's about feeling better and having more energy. You could be 110 pounds, but not eating healthily, so you're always tired and weak. Or you could be 160 pounds, eating good whole foods, and feeling great with plenty of stamina.

We often lose sight of the fact that we need to care about what we eat for more important reasons than simply looking good, losing weight, or getting ready for swimsuit season. Rather, our primary goals should be teaching our children to eat wisely, having the energy to take care of our family, and staying healthy so we can stick around long enough to see our grandchildren run our children ragged. Obviously, there are times, for health reasons, when we need to cut back a bit and lose some weight. And we should be eating healthily all the time, no matter how much we weigh. (I consider healthy eating to include the occasional indulgence!)

With this in mind, I've collected a handful of healthy eating tips to share with you in the next Rest Stop.

Healthy Eating—Rest Stop
God on Weight: Wait on God

 ## A Taste of Honey

I am eager to share some practical, daily "tricks" that help keep me on my long-term healthy eating goals. But first, the number one, most effective "trick" is actually more of a "treat." Eat lots of honey! (Remember our earlier chapter on Bible Study.) Too often we attempt to fill up the empty places inside our souls with things that will never satisfy. These can be obviously destructive like drugs, alcohol, and sex outside of marriage, to name a few. As Christians, we know these aren't pleasing to the Lord, so instead we turn to more "acceptable" alternatives like spending money we don't have, working too many hours, or overeating.

Before you switch to more nutritional eating habits or embark on a healthy weight-loss program, make sure you are filling up with Jesus first. You might be surprised how much easier it is to eat right when you find your satisfaction, first and foremost, in the Lord.

Set aside time to wait on God and delight in Him. He will not only give you the desires of your heart, but He will also take away the cravings of your soul, which often result in feeding the flesh.

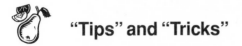

"Tips" and "Tricks"

❖ Drink a big glass of water before each meal. This tricks your body into thinking it is fuller than it really is.

❖ When tempted to eat, brush your teeth. This one really works for me!

❖ Never eat standing up. That is a telltale sign that you might be snacking on something you shouldn't.

Plan Ahead

❖ Make your lunch when you make your kids' lunches. It will keep you from getting busy and not eating, only to splurge later on a Big Mac while running errands or picking the kids up at school or activities.

❖ Pack your lunch for workdays. (Leftovers are perfect!) You have a ready excuse if asked to go out with co-workers, keeping you from being tempted with foods not consistent with your goals. It also saves lots of money—which you can pool into a "slush fund" for that new pair of jeans or a pedicure.

❖ Buy low-fat or sugar-free treats that are yours alone. (Not that the kids are really going to be wrestling you for these.)

❖ Cut up lots of fruits or veggies as soon as you get home from the grocery store and pack them in snack-sized sandwich bags. Having handy, portable healthy snacks available will keep you from grabbing the unhealthy alternative.

❖ Keep healthy snacks at your workplace to cure hunger pangs before lunch or dinner. You don't spend your money or calories on junk from the vending machine, and it keeps you from binging at mealtime because you are "starving."

Eating Out

❖ When eating out, select restaurants you know offer healthy choices. For instance, if you are low on willpower, don't choose an Italian or Mexican restaurant. If you must eat at a higher-calorie, less-healthy restaurant, decide ahead of time what you are going to order. Don't even open the menu. Order a grilled chicken salad with the dressing on the side, or chicken fajitas without the sour cream and guacamole. I don't know what to tell you about the chips and garlic bread. Perhaps you could imagine maggots crawling all over them or something.

❖ Eat half of anything. Steve and I use this one a lot. We split a meal, each eating only half. This also works great with children who are too big for kids' meals but not quite old enough for large portions.

❖ If you're ordering a full entrée, just eat half and save the other half for later! Ask for a box when you order, and then as soon as you get your meal, put half of it in the to-go box so you won't be tempted to nibble.

❖ If you are catching a meal on the run, choose places with healthy offerings, like Subway or Chick-fil-A, or a drive-thru with great salads.

Dining at Home

❖ If you can't eat it, don't buy it! If you want the kids to have some "treats" occasionally that aren't super healthy, buy stuff for them that you don't like. And keep lots of healthy treats in ready view and reach for the kids. After all, it doesn't do them any favors to learn to eat unhealthy foods, as they'll end up with the same struggle later in life you may be dealing with now!

❖ Don't finish the food on your child's plate! Save it for later, or throw it out.

❖ Make popsicles with Kool-Aid mix and Splenda or Stevia to use as treats instead of less-healthful choices.

❖ Eat as "close to the garden" as you can. This could also be "eat as close to the farm" or "as close to the sea" as you can. This means whole foods and fresh foods are always better than processed foods. Rather than Hamburger Helper, serve small portions of red beef with whole grain rice or red potatoes, plus a fresh salad or other raw vegetable. Rather than chicken cooked in a rich cream sauce, stir-fry it with fresh vegetables with little or no oil and spices. Add fish, not just fish sticks, which is more readily available than ever, to your family's weekly menu, and serve it with lots of fresh vegetables and whole grains.

 ## Moderation Is the Key

❖ Fad diets don't work—they never have and they never will. Changing your eating habits and developing a healthy lifestyle will work, though it will take a lot of time. I can tell you from firsthand experience, I've been dieting since I was twelve years old, and I have ALWAYS gained any weight back that I lost on a fad diet. Unless you simply want to look good for a family portrait, high school reunion, or swimsuit competition—don't waste your time.

❖ Moderation is the key to everything, particularly when it comes to making healthy eating choices. If you go to a wedding and your goals say "no cake," but you just can't resist, then have only a couple of bites rather than filling your plate with both bride and groom's cakes, nuts, mints, and sugary punch! Prepare your heart ahead of time and ask the Lord to help you make good choices.

❖ If sweets are your temptation, then decide beforehand how much you will allow yourself, and stick to it. If that's "one sweet thing" every day, then you can have a candy bar, but no sugary soda. Or one scoop of ice cream, but not a root beer float, unless you use diet root beer. Begin to curb your cravings and build discipline, and making good choices will get progressively easier!

❖ This "sweets" approach above can be used for anything you crave. Decide to only have mashed potatoes once a week. Or only one starch each day, or red meat only twice each week, etc.

❖ Because I'm an "all or nothing" kind of girl, I have created my own twist on moderation. I tackle one bad eating habit at a time. For example, I will spend one whole month cleansing my system of sugar. When the month is over, I try to slowly add it back into my diet—in moderation. The next month, I'll abstain from white flour, then carbonated sodas, etc. Purging the toxins out of my system makes it easier for me to then attempt a more balanced diet.

Food Journaling

The old adage, "The beginning of the solution is recognizing the problem" is true when it comes to healthy eating. This area is one that is so unique to each person and to each family. That is why I believe starting with a food journal is so important. You will be amazed at just how insightful this exercise is!

The concept is simple. Just get a spiral notebook dedicated to the purpose, and one morning, begin entering everything you eat during the day. In addition to the amount and food, write down the time you ate it and if there was a particular reason. Don't be surprised when "hungry" doesn't turn out to be the real reason you're eating sometimes. If you are concerned about your family's eating habits, try to capture the family's daily intake as well.

Do this for a week, and then go back and examine the data. The Lord will help you see unhealthy patterns and times when emotions were driving the intake rather than need or your nutritional goals.

 ## Weight-Loss Programs

There are several good Bible-based weight-loss programs that offer support and encouragement toward both weight goals and healthy eating. If you need support in this area, don't be afraid of joining with brothers and sisters of faith who are struggling in the same area. Solicit a friend to begin with you. Statistics show an amazing rise in success if you embark on a program with a friend. Having a set schedule/appointment where you plan to deal with the issues each week or month can be great incentive in and of itself! Here's a list of some of the most popular ones, but you can find additional info via the Internet or your Christian bookstore:

The Maker's Diet (Siloam Press, 2004)

Lose It for Life (Integrity Publishers, 2004)

First Place (Gospel Light, 2001)

There are also great "secular" weight-loss programs out there, like Weight Watchers and Jenny Craig. But remember—what you have always heard about weight-loss programs is true: you should always consult a doctor before embarking on any program. You should also check out the program you decide to use thoroughly before making changes, particularly dramatic changes.

I'm sitting here in the family room eating a bagel with cream cheese. I'm so sore at this very minute that even the movement of my fingertips typing across my laptop keyboard is making me wince. You see, yesterday, Clancy and I took our first stretching and resistance class at our local gym. I am sore in places I didn't even know I was supposed to have muscles!

I will describe my "resistance" to exercise more thoroughly in the next chapter. Until then, suffice to say, since becoming a mom, in order for me to invest the time in exercising I have to see there is a benefit in it beyond myself. Thus explains my recent experiment, exercising with a giant rubber band and a giant ball.

I joined a gym last week because my teenage daughters wanted to, and I thought it would be a way for me to spend some time doing something they enjoy. (How they can use the words "enjoy" and "exercise" in the same sentence, I'll never know.) Needless to say, this new routine is stretching me in more ways than one. You know what's really odd? I actually feel good about feeling so bad.

10

Exercise

How to Be More Energy Efficient

I hate to exercise! I don't enjoy it, I don't have time, and I don't care to produce endorphins, thank you very much. (They sound like something between a witch and a shark, to me.) Besides, I started exercising young, so I think I should be able to retire from it early. From the time I was twelve years old and a Mouseketeer on *The New Mickey Mouse Club*, I've been exercising to lose weight.

I remember filming at Disneyland and running from one end of the park to the next every night in order to log my requisite number of daily miles. It hardly ever rains in Southern California, but when it did, I would run around in a circle in our parking garage below my apartment. I suppose, you can surmise, there was an awful lot of pressure on me to exercise every day if I wanted to compete in Hollywood.

After I grew up and left show business to concentrate on being a full-time wife and mother, I gladly left my spandex pants and sports bra behind. For one thing, there was no way those tiny pants could have stretched to cover the "baby fat" I put on while preg-nant. Plus, I needed the bra with the handy-dandy little open-and-close flap for nursing.

For years I refused to set foot on any exercise apparatus, near a gym floor, or into running shoes, except for comfort. Then something happened: I started getting old and tired and run down. My youthful energy betrayed me. My metabolism started slowing down about the same time my children started doing the same thing. I was no longer running after them all day. Pretty soon I was approaching my second trimester weight, and I wasn't even pregnant!

I begrudgingly purchased a treadmill and hopped on for the first time in years. You're not going to believe what happened: I loved it! Well, maybe *love* is a strong word. I tolerated it, and there were even days when I didn't hate it. I used to exercise because I had to; now I do it because I want to. I still don't have time, but I try to make time. The truth is, when I exercise I have more energy so I'm less sluggish and ultimately use my time more efficiently.

The apostle Paul knew the importance of keeping his body in shape as well as his spirit. In 1 Corinthians 9:27, he says, "I discipline my body like an athlete, training it to do what it should. Otherwise, I fear that after preaching to others I myself might be disqualified" (NLT). (Actually, I prefer the ASV translation that reads, "I buffet my body." I would much rather take my body to Luby's Cafeteria and Buffet.)

Hebrews 10:36 says, "For you have need of endurance, so that when you have done the will of God you may receive what is promised." Remember what I said at the beginning: our body, soul, and spirit all work together. We need endurance to steadfastly obey God *and* to run after our little ones all day. We must discipline our bodies to resist temptation *and* to prevent osteo-porosis. We must run the race to win the prize of the eternal crown (1 Corinthians 9:25), *and* we must run to keep our heart healthy so we can live a long, good life. It's not just about looking good and having a hard body; it's about taking care of the "me" in mommy by keeping in shape—body, soul, and spirit!

Remember, exercise is to promote your long-term health. A healthier you means a happier you, a longer-living you, and a more energetic you. It's a win-win situation—you feel better, and your family reaps the benefits of a healthier mom!

I've discovered a way to multi-task while exercising and accomplish many goals at the same time. For example, I put on my headphones, plug in my contemporary Christian music, and focus on worshiping God. Even with the music blaring, God seems to talk to me more on the treadmill than any other time of the day—even more than my quiet time. Go figure!

Allow me to share a few little tips that have helped me. First thing in the morning, I crawl out of bed and put on my sports bra, old T-shirt, sweat-pants, and running shoes. Before I get dressed for the day, I say to myself, "Just get on the treadmill for twenty minutes. You can certainly spare twenty minutes. You're all dressed for it anyway."

Call it a head game, mind psyche, or brainwashing; it doesn't matter. I inevitably stay on the treadmill for longer than twenty minutes (not much longer, but longer), and I still have time to shower and get on with my day. Some days I really don't have more time, but by not allowing myself to hop in the shower until I've hopped on the treadmill, at least I've accomplished a little.

Another trick I've learned is to exercise with a friend. For a while, my mom and I worked out at a gym together. I love spending time with my mom, so even talking while lifting weights was a treat. (At least for the first few repetitions.) Nowadays, Haven and I regularly play racquetball together. I had been praying and asking the Lord to show me something special I could do and share with each child as he or she is getting older. It has been such fun having my pants beat off by my little girl. (Or maybe they are just falling off because I'm working off so many inches!)

Perhaps you've heard the verse that says, "Bodily exercise profits a little, but godliness is profitable for all things, having promise of the life that now is and of that which is to come" (1 Timothy 4:8 NKJV). I must reluctantly admit that exercise has profited me more than a little. I feel healthier, look better, and act nicer when I regularly exercise.

If you, like me, are "exercise challenged," then you need to change your perspective. Exercise is a chance to do something for yourself! Don't see it as a waste of time; think of it as an investment in yourself, your quality of life, and the way you're going to feel all day. You are going to have the energy to give your family all that is in your heart to give.

So, since you can't join me at the gym, why don't you join me at the next Rest Stop? I'll share some more tips I've learned for making exercise a regular and fun part of your week.

Exercise—Rest Stop
Get Moving and Have Fun

 Make It Fun

For fellow "exercise haters," here are some tips for keeping the allotted time bearable:

❖ Do a different activity each day. Monday you could swim, Tuesday could be a nice evening walk, Wednesday could be the treadmill, and so on. This may help you think of the time as an activity rather than "I have to exercise."

❖ Make your exercise environment pleasant. Who wants to go in the closet and exercise? In good weather, put the treadmill on the porch. Many treadmills roll on wheels, and you'll enjoy the change, making it worth the extra effort.

❖ Don't walk faster than you can hold a magazine or book and read. I used to restrain myself from reading my scrapbook magazines when they came in the mail so I would look forward to getting on the stationary bike.

❖ Walk on the treadmill during your favorite television show.

❖ Rent a favorite DVD and watch a bit every day while exercising. With longer rental times, you should be able to finish the entire movie before you have to return it.

 ## Play Mind Games

❖ Don't focus on the exercise time itself. Think about how refreshed you will feel when you're done—and how successful you will feel at the accomplishment. Ask the Lord to help you enjoy your time. Attitude is everything—you can choose to like it or not. Be positive about exercising, and see if your attitude doesn't start reflecting the choice.

❖ Next time you really feel like taking a nap, force yourself to exercise instead. Naps are great, but sometimes you wake up feeling more sluggish than when you lay down. That definitely won't happen if you take a ten-minute "power jog," even if it is in one place.

 ## Time Crunchers

Can't fit exercise into your life? Here's some ways to squeeze time out of thin air:

❖ Use your lunch break to go to a gym near work.

❖ While kids are at baseball or football practice, walk around the track or parking lot.

❖ Exercise before Dad leaves the house in the morning. Have him allow fifteen extra minutes for getting ready, so he can take care of the kids in case anything comes up.

❖ Do arm lifts with plastic grocery bags as you're bringing them in from the car.

❖ When you shop, park at the outer edge of the parking lot. Your kids will love the buggy ride, and you can add a few more feet to your pedometer.

 ## Multitask

Believe exercise is not worth the time investment at this season of your life? Consider these options for being productive while you exercise:

❖ Take walks in the evening with your husband, kids, or another mom in the neighborhood. What better way to spend your time than investing in conversations and nurturing relationships?

❖ Organize a neighborhood "stroller brigade." This works with infants just before nap time if they enjoy the ride and will sleep in a stroller.

❖ Tape or TiVo TV shows and save them for exercise times. By skipping the commercials, you can actually save time watching them and get your exercise too.

❖ Listen to a Bible CD or a great teaching tape while exercising.

❖ Activities spent with the kids (bike riding, roller blading, trampoline, etc.) can be much more about spending quality time together and having fun than exercise!

❖ Watch the morning news shows while you exercise, so you can have adult conversation with your hubby about the stories later.

❖ Mow the lawn. It's great for muscles, and you have the added benefit of getting a little sun—and a manicured lawn. (Hey, at least something should get a manicure if you can't.)

❖ Have sex! Would you rather find a baby-sitter, get dressed in your workout clothes, and run a mile three times a week or put your kids to bed, get undressed, and have sex with your husband six nights a week? They both burn the same amount of calories, but only one of them strengthens your body and your marriage.

 ## Jump-Start Your Exercise Routine

When you need extra motivation, here are some ideas for jump-starting your routine:

❖ Hire a personal trainer. I know, this sounds like something only rich and famous people do. But there are students who need the practice, and you can split the time with friends by having a trainer coach you as a group. Many gyms also offer very brief sessions with personal trainers at a reduced rate.

❖ Join a gym. Many gyms offer free child care which is a huge bonus! I recently joined "Curves." I love this gym because I can get in and out in less than thirty minutes, having covered both cardio-vascular and strength training. My favorite thing is the fact that most of the other ladies exercising beside me look like me, rather than perfect "10s."

❖ Purchase a new workout video. My good friend Stormie Omartian has some really great ones! (If you look closely, you will see me almost twenty years and twenty pounds ago.)

 ## Try Something New!

Don't get stuck in a rut! Try something new when you exercise—remember, it is your health that you are investing in. Vary your exercise routine with some of these great exercises:

- ❖ Taebo

- ❖ Karate (good for goal setters)

- ❖ Kickboxing

- ❖ Weight training (you can do this at home—use canned goods for weights and rent a training video)

- ❖ Resistance training

- ❖ Step exercise

- ❖ Mini-trampoline (or go jump with the kids on the big one!)

- ❖ Exercise ball (resistance)

- ❖ Aquatics

- ❖ Jazzercise

- ❖ Marathon training (same as karate—for the "overmotivated"!)

- ❖ Bicycling (ride with the kids—you get double pleasure and productivity)

- ❖ Dancing (doesn't have to be formal—just put on some great music and dance around the house with the kids)

- ❖ Jumping rope (But be careful! I tried this and couldn't walk for three days because my calves were so cramped up, I couldn't "mooo-ve" them.)

- ❖ Rollerblading

- ❖ Hiking

We've found ways to nourish our spirit and feed our bodies (healthy food, of course.) Now it's time to discover new ideas for nurturing our souls. In the next chapter, I share what is probably the most vulnerable story I've ever written. The reason I've chosen this time and this book to reveal this particular struggle is because of the life-changing lesson I learned having gone through it.

I pray you will discern the gravity of the need to pay attention as closely to your mind as you do your spirit and body.

**part
3**

Taking Care of Your Soul

Your Soul

Keep a Girdle on That Mind

*T*he definition I chose for *soul* in the introduction of this book clarified that it refers "to the will, the emotions, and the reason." In this section of the book, I want to offer ways for you to strengthen your will in the area of finances, express your emotions through fun and hobbies, and exercise your reasoning capacities by keeping your brain in shape. Tending your soul is critical to your spiritual, emotional, mental, and physical health.

I'm so passionate about this book and the importance of strengthening not only our spirits but also our bodies and souls. With Steve's blessing, I want to share a very personal illustration with you.

I had three babies in diapers, had lost all the money I made on *The Facts of Life*, and was living in a rental home on a pastor's salary with a man I didn't recognize as the groom I married. I was convinced the deterioration of our marriage was all my husband's fault, and he, for one, was not interested in changing.

My mind was tilling with thoughts of anger, pride, hurt,

control, unforgiveness, and hopelessness. Into this compost, seeds of discontent and comparison were sown. Eventually, a fallow friendship with another man took root in my mind and threatened to produce deadly fruit.

I've spent the first portion of this book prioritizing the importance of feeding our spirits. I wholeheartedly believe that authentic, abundant life comes from the Spirit of God as He breathes into our spirit (Genesis 2:7). No question, to sustain life we must certainly nourish our spirits. At the same time, we must be careful to prevent death from potentially breeding in our souls.

James 1:14–15 says, "Each one is tempted when he is drawn away by his own desires and enticed. Then, when desire has conceived, it gives birth to sin; and sin, when it is full-grown, brings forth death" (NKJV). Death begins in the soul, when our mind, emotion, or will is distracted from God onto something else that promises life.

Gee, I really enjoy talking with this guy is not necessarily a sinful thought. *I wonder when I'll get to see him again* is treading on dangerous ground. At first, I allowed questionable thoughts to linger in my mind because, taken at face value, there was nothing overtly sinful about them.

The problem was, when I dared look beyond this innocent contemplation in either direction, whether deeper to the root of the thought or further down the road to its logical conclusion, it wasn't so innocuous. By examining my heart, I could see that the enticement of friendly conversation with this man was actually a desire for connection with someone other than my husband, and ultimately an attempt to fill a vacuum that only God could satisfy completely. As a result, if I continued to harbor these risky reflections, I could easily wake up and find myself gambling with my marriage, testimony, and integrity.

The red flag that finally got my attention was the day I caught myself thinking about this other man in the middle of singing worship songs to my heavenly Father. It scared me. I may have been too weak and duped to fight this battle of the mind for my husband, but Satan overplayed his hand when he tried to get in between me and my Lord.

It was time to declare war. Ephesians 6:11–17 told me what I needed to do:

> Put on the whole armor of God, that you may be able to stand against the wiles of the devil. For we do not wrestle against flesh and blood, but against principalities, against powers, against the rulers of the darkness of this age, against spiritual hosts of wickedness in the heavenly places. Therefore take up the whole armor of God, that you may be able to withstand in the evil day, and having done all, to stand.
>
> Stand therefore, having girded your waist with truth, having put on the breastplate of righteousness, and having shod your feet with the preparation of the gospel of peace; above all, taking the shield of faith with which you will be able to quench all the fiery darts of the wicked one. And take the helmet of salvation, and the sword of the Spirit, which is the word of God. (NKJV)

The weapons I used most in this fight were the girdle of truth, the helmet of salvation, and the sword of the Spirit. My main objectives were to keep the helmet of salvation protecting my mind while I was fighting the enemy with the truth of God's Word.

Because I was still in the enticement and drawing-away phase, I looked up every scripture I could find on temptation and wrote them on index cards. One of my favorite verses was 2 Peter 2:9: "The Lord knows how to deliver the godly out of temptations" (NKJV).

Of course, I took some practical steps, but as Paul reminds us, we wrestle not against flesh and blood. Whenever I couldn't avoid being in a situation with this person, I would arm myself with my index cards, bulk up before the encounter by fasting, and ask a trusted friend to pray. I'm happy to report that it has been more than a decade since the enemy was defeated in this skirmish, but I dare not let down my guard.

Be especially careful about temptation during this season of motherhood. Deuteronomy 25:18 cautions us, "They attacked you when you were exhausted and weary, and they struck down those who were lagging behind" (NLT). (Sounds like the definition of a mom to me.) Take this book seriously, and start taking care of yourself. Get some rest and refreshing, set up support systems of friends and family, and strengthen your "Jesus muscles" by exercising your spirit.

Whether you are resisting inappropriate thoughts of another man, struggling with suffocating fear, wrestling through worry, overcome with cravings, squashing painful memories, or contending with guilt, the battleground is your soul and the front line of the war is your mind. Whether you win or lose is determined by where your thoughts linger.

My all-time favorite book is *Celebration of Discipline* by Richard Foster.[14] Years ago, when I first read the book and learned the importance of meditation, I thought he was referring to candles and incense and humming. Fortunately, it is a lot less esoteric than that. Wesbter's New Pocket dictionary defines *meditation* as "think deeply." That just about sums it up!

The prophet Isaiah says of God: "You will keep in perfect peace all who trust in you, whose thoughts are fixed on you!" (26:3 NLT). Meditation is a powerful tool for clearing your mind of things that distract from God and for fixing your focus on those things He approves.

In his letter to the Christians in Philippi, the apostle Paul tells us what kinds of thoughts God approves: "Whatever things are true, whatever things are noble, whatever things are just, whatever things are pure, whatever things are lovely, whatever things are of good report, if there is any virtue and if there is anything praiseworthy—meditate on these things" (Philippians 4:8 NKJV).

The following Rest Stop will, in practical ways, show you that meditation is easier than you might think.

Your Soul—Rest Stop
Meditate on This

 Meditate on Scripture

This Book of the Law shall not depart from your mouth, but you shall meditate on it day and night, so that you may be careful to do according to all that is written in it. For then you will make your way prosperous, and then you will have good success.
Joshua 1:8

❖ Ask the Lord to divinely allow a scripture to "pop out" at you during your morning devotions, and then chew on that Word and concept throughout the day. Capture it in your journal and then spend time going back over the last week or month's journal entries and allow the Lord to sink the messages in deeper.

❖ Keep a Bible by your nightstand. Choose one scripture and say it aloud as you go to bed. Fall asleep meditating on that verse.

❖ Choose a key passage of Scripture and meditate on various parts of it all day. For instance, Philippians 4:8 is a long list of virtues.

Spend a week or two with one day devoted to each virtue so that passage becomes a part of your heart and life.

❖ Find a good Internet resource and have a devotional or "Word of the Day" sent to you each morning. Use it as your meditation for the day, pondering the message in the midst of the busyness. Here are a few websites I found:

www.devotions.org

www.purposedrivenlife.com

www.cfdevotionals.org

 ## Meditate on God

I will ponder all your work, and meditate on your mighty deeds.
Psalm 77:12

❖ Fill a blank month calendar with nothing other than God's attributes and characteristics: faithful, loving , omniscient, all-powerful, wonderful, counselor, mighty, Prince of Peace, Lion of Judah, Jehovah Jireh, Jehovah Rapha . . . the list can go on and on. Then, each day, spend the entire day reflecting on that particular attribute of God and what it means to you. Choose one hymn or praise song and sing it all day long. Allow it to seep into the very fabric of your soul. Contemplate each word or phrase. If you have time, use it for your Bible study and find the scriptural basis for the lyrics.

Meditate on Thoughts from Others

Till I come, give attention to reading, to exhortation, to doctrine. Do not neglect the gift that is in you, which was given to you by prophecy with the laying on of the hands of the eldership. Meditate on these things; give yourself entirely to them, that your progress may be evident to all.

1 Timothy 4:13–15 NKJV

❖ Listen to sermons and teaching whenever you can. Don't just listen once, but let the Lord show you which messages need to "get in deeper." Repetitive listening does this, and you'll be surprised at how many times you can hear something completely new on the second or third time through. You can find many amazing sermons to download from the Internet. Visit a ministry or church site you trust and look for sermons to purchase or download for free. Here are a few resources I've discovered:

Christians Unite (http://sermons.christiansunite.com)

Sermon Audio (www.sermonaudio.com)

Higher Praises
(http://www.higherpraise.com/InspirationalBible.htm)

❖ Who are some of your favorite contemporary preachers, teachers, and authors? Chances are they have sermons available to download at no, or minimal, cost on their personal or church Web sites. Here are some I've discovered:

Ed Young (www.fellowshipchurch.com)

Rob Bell (www.mhbcmi.org/listen/index.php)

John Piper (www.preachingthebible.com)

Tony Evans (www.tonyevans.org)

❖ Read classic sermons and meditate on them. Many of them require meditation to understand because they are soooooo deep. But they are worth the extra effort. You can find everything you could ever want to learn about at Christians Unite (http://articles.christiansunite.com).

❖ Read some of the classics in Christian literature to find inspiration and deeper thoughts to ponder. Consider these authors:

❖ Oswald Chambers	❖ Charles Colson
❖ C. S. Lewis	❖ A. W. Tozer
❖ Jack Hayford	❖ Elisabeth Elliot
❖ Francis Schaeffer	❖ J. I. Packer
❖ Ron Mehl	❖ Phil Yancey
❖ John Piper	❖ Jonathan Edwards

 # Scriptures to Combat Negative Thoughts and Conversations

Finally, brothers, whatever is true, whatever is honorable, whatever is just, whatever is pure, whatever is lovely, whatever is commendable, if there is any excellence, if there is anything worthy of praise, think about these things.

Philippians 4:8

Learn how our minds control our thought patterns and proactively work to combat the negative, humanistic, or enemy-oriented thoughts with scriptures and decisions/choices to meditate on what is good, instead. When you recognize your thoughts resting or wallowing on any of the following emotions, make a disciplined choice to meditate on the corresponding scripture.

Anger

Know this, my beloved brothers: let every person be quick to hear, slow to speak, slow to anger; for the anger of man does not produce the righteousness that God requires.

James 1:19–20

Worry/Anxiety

Do not be anxious about anything, but in everything by prayer and supplication with thanksgiving let your requests be made known to God. And the peace of God, which surpasses all understanding, will guard your hearts and your minds in Christ Jesus.

Philippians 4:6–7

Bitterness

See to it that no one fails to obtain the grace of God; that no "root of bitterness" springs up and causes trouble, and by it many become defiled.

Hebrews 12:15

Self-Pity

Delight yourself in the LORD, and he will give you the desires of your heart. Commit your way to the LORD; trust in him, and he will act.

Psalm 37:4–5

Depression

> We are afflicted in every way, but not crushed; perplexed,
> but not driven to despair; persecuted, but not forsaken;
> struck down, but not destroyed.
> *2 Corinthians 4:8–9*

Fear

> For you did not receive the spirit of slavery to fall back into fear, but
> you have received the Spirit of adoption as sons,
> by whom we cry, "Abba! Father!"
> *Romans 8:15*

Hate

> Whoever says he is in the light and hates his brother is still in dark-
> ness. Whoever loves his brother abides in the light, and in him there is
> no cause for stumbling. But whoever hates his brother is in the dark-
> ness and walks in the darkness, and does not know where he is going,
> because the darkness has blinded his eyes.
> *1 John 2:9–11*

Self-Centeredness

> Let no one seek his own good, but the good of his neighbor.
> *1 Corinthians 10:24*

In many people's minds, meditation has a very real New Age feel to it. It is sad that, once again, the enemy has successfully stolen a practice that is meant to draw us closer to God and turned it into something completely different.

I have found meditation to be especially vital during this busy season of my life as a mom. I don't know if it is because I hear, "Momma, Mom, Mommy, and Mother!" in my ear all day long, or because I'm always talking, or simply too busy to take time to listen. Whatever the reason, it seems to me that I hear God speak to me most often when I quiet my heart long enough to meditate on something He's said. For me, meditation is about inclining my ear and listening to God.

There are hundreds of books written on prayer. Most of them concentrate on half of the story. Prayer is the beginning of a two-way conversation. Anyone who is in a close relationship knows the critical importance listening plays in the art of communication. If you want to hear from God, I highly recommend you cultivate the practice of inclining your ear and thinking deeply about what He says. If you are interested in learning even more, may I recommend a book by Jim Downing, entitled *Meditation.*

I hope this chapter and Rest Stop is just the beginning for you. Make it a lifestyle to combat negative thoughts and emotions with Philippians 4:8 thoughts. Protect your mind, heart, marriage, family, and every other vulnerable place of attack by girding up your mind with the belt of truth. Quiet the cacophony around you by straining to discern the still, small voice of the Lord through intentional listening.

We've talked about protecting our mind; now it is time to feed it. Did the same thing happen to you that happened to me? About the same time I started getting soft around the edges, my brain started to lose some of its sharpness too.

We are inundated with books, commercials, and remedies for feeding our bodies healthy food and strengthening our muscles. How is it that the biggest muscle of all, the brain, is left out of all the diet and exercise regimes? I think it is time to get our brains back in shape!

Mind

Feed Your Brain

My educational experience is less than stellar. I went to one of the lowest-ranking public schools in our area for kindergarten through sixth grade. I absolutely loved school, but I wouldn't say I received a college prep education. In seventh grade, I moved to Los Angeles to be on *The New Mickey Mouse Club*. I brought my schoolbooks with me and was tutored on the set when not filming the show. That was a joke. I spent most of the time reading the Judy Blume books my fellow Mouseketeer Shawnte brought from home.

When that show was cancelled, I remained in Hollywood auditioning for various shows and occasionally filming guest spots and movies that went straight to video. I don't even remember what I did for school during this time. I can't imagine that my mom allowed me to simply drop out, but I didn't have any defined school routine.

I do know that it was during this time that my mother found a Christian school in Fort Worth that was testing a new curriculum that looked like the perfect answer. There were about sixty students in the high school, and they all met in one room, with dividers separating the workspaces. One teacher was available to answer questions and explain any instructions that weren't clear, while each student worked independently on their packets. (I discovered years later that we were actually using a homeschool curriculum.)

I was able to take these packets with me to California and teach myself for about a year. Then I got the part on *The Facts of Life*, so I had a tutor on the set again. I continued working, pretty much independently, on the curriculum from the Christian school in Fort Worth. By law, child actors are required to go to school on the set for three hours a day. We went four hours a day, so we could "bank" some time in order to work all day on taping days.

Just before we were to begin taping the second season of the show, the actors' union went on strike, so filming was suspended for a total of six months. I used this break to go back home to Texas and enjoy life as a typical teenager. I attended the Christian school, made friends, got involved in the church youth group, went on dates, and went to football games and pizza parties and had the time of my life.

I also used this time to get ahead in my schoolwork. Back in California, I was tired of being in the studio trailer half the day while a stand-in read my lines for me and learned the blocking for me in the rehearsal hall. So I made an appointment with the school principal and asked him if I could double up on the number of packets I was doing so I could graduate high school before I went back to work. He gave me the OK, so I finished my last two years of high school in six months. Now I was free to return to California and actually do what I was hired to do and loved doing.

To be honest with you, I don't remember much of anything I learned in school. Most of what I've actually needed in life, I've learned by living and traveling and reading—lots and lots of reading. I used to read on the set so much that the other girls got frustrated with me and confronted me in my dressing room one day about how rude I was being as an actress. They were right. I should have at least put my book down longer than to simply say my line and stick my nose back in it.

I was such a voracious reader that I was in for some serious withdrawal after I had children. I couldn't find a minute to read! And whenever I tried to open a book, I fell asleep before I could even read a paragraph. I didn't have the time or energy to work the logic and word puzzles I always enjoyed either. My *Games* magazines gave way to *Christian Parenting*, and *Pride and Prejudice* was replaced by *Clifford, the Big Red Dog.* My brain began thinking in one-syllable, short-vowel words. (If I could remember the word at all.)

You know it is bad when your sentences start sounding like this: "Honey, will you hand me that doohickey over there on that thingy next to the watchamacallit?" I don't remember if it was before or after I lost a game of Speed Scrabble to a ten-year-old, but I knew it was time to start feeding and exercising my brain before it shriveled up and died. Not just for my own good but also for the good of my family.

Proverbs 24:3 says, "By wisdom a house is built, and by understanding it is established." I wanted to know the difference between *wisdom* and *understanding,* so I did a quick word study and discovered that wisdom is often associated with spiritual knowledge and insight, whereas understanding is personified as an intelligent teacher.

I also looked up the difference between *built* and *established.* The word *built* is talking about making and creating something. The definition of *established* in the original Greek includes words like *furnish, arrange, provide,* and *prepare.* This scripture uses the analogy of a house, which is perfect. We set our house on a firm foundation by building it on the wisdom of the Lord. With understanding, we make our house a home as we continue to grow and learn and pass this wisdom on to our children.

I love the verse that immediately follows these instructions: "By knowledge the rooms are filled with all precious and pleasant riches." I believe this passage proves it. Our families will be blessed as we seek the Lord and continue to grow in knowledge and understanding. So, as Proverbs 4:7 says so perfectly, "Wisdom is the principal thing; Therefore get wisdom. And in all your getting, get understanding" (NKJV).

If you, too, have found yourself "losing your mind," then hopefully you'll find some ideas in the next Rest Stop to encourage you to take care of your brain, as well as your body and spirit. As Proverbs 15:14 says, "The heart of him who has understanding seeks knowledge" (NKJV).

Since our brains are hiding, let's go seek!

Feed Your Brain—Rest Stop Synapse Snacks

All of us realize the need to avoid getting into a rut and becoming boring to our children, our husbands . . . and ourselves! But how do we find the time to expand and explore? Here are a few of my "quick sneak-away" favorites:

❖ Libraries have kids' activities where staff check your kids in, allowing you free time to explore the library on your own. Many libraries have computers, which makes this an ideal time not only to find reading materials but to do research on hobbies or health and nutrition issues.

❖ Bring your book to soccer practice or dance lessons. Stay in the car, roll down the windows, and get lost in a book.

❖ For working moms, spend your lunch hours and breaks enjoying some mind stimulation.

❖ Read while exercising on a stationary bike or walking on a treadmill. You can purchase book holders to attach to your exercise equipment to make this easier.

❖ Consider "fasting" from a favorite TV show for a season. Instead of spending that time watching TV, find a fun book or series of books to read aloud as a family.

❖ If you sit down to relax and watch TV and the show is a rerun, take that as a cue that it's time to read or play a game instead.

❖ Keep magazines or newspapers in a tote bag or the seat pocket of your car so you can catch an article here and there. *Reader's Digest* is good for this, since it's compact and very diverse. Even their "Word Power" quizzes are fun and can be done in just a few minutes. *Guideposts* is also a good choice. With these small, portable stimulators, you can read everywhere—in the long grocery line, the post office, while you are stuck in traffic waiting for an accident to clear, when your kids' practice is running a little late. It turns these frustrating moments into welcome interruptions as you catch a few minutes to exercise your brain.

 **Reading**

Personally, reading is my favorite "dish for the brain." When my kids were tiny, I thought I would shrivel up for lack of time to read. Here are a few ideas to get some "word nutrition:"

❖ Consider organizing a monthly book club. There are Web sites devoted to ideas for making it fun, but the general idea is that everyone in the group reads the same book, then you get together for discussion and fun. For step-by-step instructions visit www.ehow.com and type "book club" in the search window. (By the way, this is a fascinating Web site. You can even sign up to have a "How-To" tip emailed to you daily.)

❖ Even if it's only reading one novel or play a year, find time to expand your mind with a time-tested favorite, or select a favorite from your childhood. Some fun, easy books that can be read in short spurts include *Charlotte's Web, Little House on the Prairie, Nancy Drew* mysteries, *The Chronicles of Narnia,* and many others. You can also read these books aloud to your children while they are coloring, painting, or playing quietly.

❖ If you have a hard time "just reading" novels, books, or magazines, find a topic that is both interesting and practical to explore, such as investment strategy, computer skills, health and nutrition, planning for the upcoming family vacation, etc.

❖ If you're not an avid reader, try listening to books on tape. There are lots of great ones to choose from! You can check some out from your local library for free. Cracker Barrel restaurants also have a great program where you can rent audio books. Or look online to purchase audio books at a discount:

www.amazingaudiobookguide.com

http://www.hotaudiobooks.com

 Television

While not all of it is healthy or educational, public broadcasting stations and some cable channels do offer many historical or scientific shows that expand our minds. Check out the show listings at:

www.historychannel.com

www.discovery.com

www.aetv.com/class

www.biographychannel.com

www.pbs.org

❖ They also offer great cooking shows. And while I never expect to *actually* make most of the dishes they cook, you can learn a great deal about technique, spices, new food combinations, and food preparation by tuning in.

 **Puzzles**

❖ Puzzles of all kinds are like vitamins for the brain. You can find games online at:

www.brainbashers.com

www.brainconnection.com

www.wordplays.com

❖ *Games* magazine is one of my favorite magazines. I used to carry it with me on the set of *The Facts of Life* and work through the puzzles in between scenes. This magazine, and others like it, are great to stick in your purse or glove compartment for those "stealable" minutes.

 **Board Games**

I am an avid board and card game player. That is one of the reasons I started my MomTime group over a dozen years ago. Steve hates games and my kids were too young, so I had to find other friends to play with. I like ALL kinds of games. Here's a list of our favorite games to play at MomTime:

❖ Moods®

❖ The Poll Game®

- Worst Case Scenario®

- Channel Surfing®

- Scene-It TV Edition®

- Babble-On®

I enjoy challenging, mind-stimulating, thinking games. Here's a list of some of my favorites:

- Trivial Pursuit®

- Scrabble®

- Boggle®

- Chronology®

- Scattergories®

- Mind Trap®

- Huggermugger®

- Clever Endeavor®

 Online

- Keep a list near your computer of subjects you want to research. This can be anything from the next car you want to purchase to a natural remedy for joint pain. When you have a few minutes, do an Internet search.

- Online games—If you can be disciplined about not taking too much time for these, you can have lots of fun playing chess, backgammon, spades, and many other games on-ine alone or with a virtual friend. Check out some of these fun and mind-stretching sites:

www.tagnwag.com/games/

www.games.com

http://games.yahoo.com/

❖ You can also have teasers and questions sent to your e-mail.

www.braingle.com

❖ Have a new word sent via e-mail every day. Commit to finding a way to use this word in a sentence at least three times that day. Write it down on an index card and post it near your computer or kitchen sink. Spell it out loud until you can spell it with your eyes closed.

www.wordsmith.org

www.dictionary.com

www.mywordaday.com

www.gamesforthebrain.com (an all-around fun and fabulous site)

 ## Current Events

❖ Subscribe to a regional or national newspaper, perhaps just on the weekends. Even if all you get to read is the "At a Glance" section, you'll be able to stay in touch with many current events.

❖ Google News. This is a great resource for current news stories.

❖ *The Week* magazine. The articles are "mommy-sized," and it will give you more things to talk about with your husband: "Honey, did you read that article on immediate annuities?" (www.theweekmagazine.com)

❖ Focus on the Family Citizen Link (www.family.org/cforum). This is a great resource for keeping up to date on current issues and events from a Christian worldview.

❖ If you can afford a subscription to *USA Today*, it is a quick, colorful, enjoyable way to stay on top of the news.

Continuing Education

These next suggestions may take larger blocks of time, but the rewards are also greater! If you start by incorporating some of the quick suggestions above, you may decide you want more—so these can be used as goals for the future. Consider selecting one or two each year.

❖ Take a class. Many local stores and communities have classes or groups for these interests. They not only offer mind expansion and an opportunity for learning new, fun things, but are also a great place to make new friends with whom you can share Jesus! All of these offer new educational opportunities and a chance to expand your horizons. Have you considered a class in:

- Foreign Language

- Computer skills

- Financial Planning

- Business

- Graphic Design

- Interior Decorating

- Nutrition

- Real Estate

- Web Design

- Public Speaking

- Party Planning

❖ Stay current on the field you studied in college. Or choose a sub-ject you're really interested in and stay actively engaged in learn-ing all about it and the advances in that field. If you ever decide to go back to college for more education, you won't feel so "out of the loop." If your children are old enough, consider going back to col-lege online. Even one course a semester can keep your brain in tip-top shape.

❖ Another great way to stay in touch with classic literature and art is attending local Shakespeare festivals or college drama depart-ment productions.

❖ Homeschooling your children will certainly keep your mind engaged. I think I am learning as much as my kids are!

❖ Never underestimate how much exercise your brain is getting when you help your kids with their homework. Consider it time well spent developing your brainpower, not just theirs!

 **Spiritual Enrichment**

There are lots of ways you can expand your mind and receive spiritual benefit at the same time:

❖ Take your devotional time up a notch—try some in-depth Bible studies. If you need suggestions, ask your local church leadership, browse the Christian bookstore, or check out the Bible-reading Rest Stop on page 27.

❖ The Charles Stanley Institute for Christian Living offers online discipleship courses, as do Antioch Internet Bible Institute and Internet Bible College. Actually, most all Bible colleges and seminaries offer online classes. These courses will definitely feed your brain and your spirit. The good news is, you don't have to enroll for a grade, so if you can't find time for the homework you don't have to stress about it.

❖ Enjoy some life-changing and entertaining inspirational fiction. Some of my favorite authors are Francine Rivers, Ted Dekker, Randy Alcorn, and Brock and Bodie Thoene. (Be careful with "secular" romance novels. Not only are they extremely dangerous and can lead to unrealistic expectations or worse in your marriage relationship, they're not exactly "mind-expanding" reading anyway!)

❖ Another Christian book section to check out is biographies. There are some amazing and inspiring stories of believers whose lives have touched the world. Check them out—you can learn wonderful and valuable life lessons from these spiritual giants. Start with the following classics:

- *The Hiding Place* / Corrie ten Boom

- *Surprised by Joy* / C. S. Lewis

- *Born Again* / Charles Colson

- *The Cross and the Switchblade* / David Wilkerson

- *Through Gates of Splendor* / Elisabeth Elliot

- *A Severe Mercy* / Sheldon Vanauken

- *The Seven Storey Mountain* / Thomas Merton

- *Power of the Powerless* / Christopher de Vinck

- *Something Beautiful for God* / Malcolm Muggeridge

- *A Prophet with Honor* / William Martin

- *Joni* / Joni Eareckson

It would be a very tough call if someone made me decide what I enjoyed doing most, reading or scrapbooking. I like to think I'm feeding my mind by reading and feeding my heart with scrapbooking. I don't know. I just made that up. Whatever the reason, I know that both activities touch something deeper inside me than a simple book or hobby alone could.

I'm about to get up on my soapbox and give my speech about the godliness of hobbies. It may be a stretch for some people, but I believe it with all my heart. Please, just hear me out before you toss this book into the heresy pile.

Hobbies

Creative in God's Image

When I was a little girl, my mom sewed almost all of my clothes. She made mother/daughter outfits. I had matching clothes with my cousins. My Barbie dolls were even able to dress like me! One of my earliest memories is of waking up in the middle of the night and peeking through sleepy eyes to see my mom sitting at the sewing machine at the foot of my bed, sewing clothes for me.

It is true; we do grow up to be our mothers. (If there were ever any doubt, all I have to do is take one look at myself in the mirror as I step out of the shower.) As heredity would have it, once I had kids the DNA took over, and I was overcome with the desire to sew like the wind.

I have a wonderful friend named Gloria who, although retired, is anything but sedentary. She can do anything and everything! One Saturday, I spent the morning at her house, and she taught me how to sew. Then I bought a sewing machine and took the classes that came with the purchase. I became progressively obsessed until one day I found myself at the L.A. County fair shopping for a serger!

I used to mark my calendar for the twice-yearly 40 percent off sale at our local fabric store. I would go in the day before, choose six months' worth of patterns, pick out fabric and notions, and be ready and waiting when the doors opened the next morning.

(I was actually in a holdup once at this fabric store. I was eight months pregnant with Haven, and I had my little brother, Casey, with me. When the guy in front of me at the cash register pulled out a gun, I whispered to Casey, "Go hide in the fabric bolts." As he ran off, the gunman whirled around and pointed the gun at me and told me not to move. I just stood there, laying hands on my baby and praying for her safety. Thankfully, the guy took the money and ran.)

OK, back from that little rabbit trail. Now, where was I? Oh yeah, I was fanatically sewing everything. Curtains, cushions, purses, place mats . . . if I could have sewn a new dinette and chairs I think I would have tried. About this time my cousin, Nancy, got married. I sewed the whole family's clothes, including a maternity dress for me. But Steve refused to allow me to attempt a tuxedo. When I look back at the pictures, I'm pretty sure he made the right choice.

One of the things I loved best about the little house we were renting when my children were small was the fact that I could place my sewing table next to the sliding-glass door and watch my children play in the backyard. I spent hours "playing" in my bedroom while they played outside. Those are some of my happiest memories.

Now that I have teenagers, I can't even safely pick out my children's clothes anymore, much less sew them. So I've transferred my obsession to scrapbooking. (Although I have scrapbooked a two-page layout of matching outfits I sewed for my kids when they were little.)

When I was collecting ideas for this book, I received an e-mail from a lady who asked me, "Are hobbies really necessary?" Well, I don't know that I would deem them necessary, but I can certainly make a good case for their benefit in preserving my sanity and perhaps, consequently, my children's safety. Hobbies have definitely been a stress reliever in my life!

I think I could go so far as to say that hobbies and crafts could be considered downright godly! God's very first action in the Bible was to create. He is called our Creator. I believe it is the spirit of God within us that yearns to create and is refreshed when we exercise this character trait of creation.

In Beth Moore's Bible studies, I have learned that to glorify God means to reflect His nature. That being the case, I would answer that having a hobby may not be necessary, but what a great way to bring glory to God! "Everyone who is called by My name, whom I have created for My glory; I have formed him, yes, I have made him" (Isaiah 43:7 NKJV).

I'm wondering if maybe we didn't all inherit some of our heavenly Father's DNA and that is why we get so much joy from creative outlets like hobbies. Ask yourself this question: "Did God create nature for His pleasure or ours?" Well, Colossians 1:16 says, "All things were created by him and for him" (NIV).

The next time you feel a twinge of guilt for spending time on yourself with a hobby, remind yourself that even God likes to do a little something for Himself by exercising His creativity. And the truth is, most of the time we are creating things to give away or share with other people anyway. One more example of our Father's DNA.

In the following Rest Stop, I will share a handful of hobby suggestions and how to find time to enjoy them. I will even tell you what is God's craft of choice. Here's a hint: He talks about it in Psalm 139.

$\mathcal{H}obbies—\mathcal{R}est\ \mathcal{S}top$
$\mathcal{B}e\ a\ \mathcal{C}rafty\ \mathcal{L}ady$

Hobbies are a great way to accomplish many of the other things we've discussed: relaxation, time for you, something to give to others, and something that feeds your soul.

 ## Finding Time

❖ Hobbies don't "just happen." You have to make time for them, which, at my house, means I have to actually chart them into my schedule. For the last few years, every time Steve has asked me what I want for my birthday or Christmas, I've said the same thing: I want to go away on a scrapbook weekend retreat. When I'm at home, it is difficult for me to stay focused when the kids, laundry, e-mail, and a million other "urgent" things are competing with, what then feels like, my "silly little hobby."

Occasionally I can find time at home by following one of these ideas:

❖ Let your kids do a craft with you, and then send their creations to a soldier overseas or bring them to a local nursing home. This blesses someone else, keeps the fridge decluttered, and leaves you guilt-free since you won't have to throw your child's crafts away.

❖ If you're worried about your hobby taking time away from your family, do it during *Monday Night Football*, after the kids are in bed.

❖ Find a friend who enjoys the same hobby and set a time on the calendar to meet with her. It is so easy to say no when it comes time to doing something for yourself, but if you've obligated yourself to meet with a friend you won't be so inclined to cancel because there are so many other things you "should" be doing.

❖ Knitting, needlepoint, crocheting, and other handwork are wonderful hobbies because you can take them with you and make "down time" or delays into craft time.

❖ Once a week after everyone drops the kids off at school, collect your craft or scrapbooking supplies and meet at a friend's house to have fun until it is time to pick the kids up in the afternoon. Rotate homes, and the person who hosts that week also prepares a salad or pot of soup for all the moms.

❖ Make a date with your hobby. No, I didn't say hubby, although that is important too, but we'll talk about that in a later chapter. Put "craft times" on your calendar.

Hobbies Can Be Productive

Here are some hobby ideas for those of you who need to be convinced hobbies aren't just a waste of time. These can serve double purposes and be productive:

❖ Cooking is a great hobby for the practical-minded. Older children can learn useful skills while you develop your creations.

❖ Cake-decorating classes can be a really fun and even profitable hobby. But be careful: when I was little, my mom took a class and gained fifteen pounds!

❖ Make Christmas gifts throughout the year for holiday giving.

❖ Take up gardening as a hobby. I can't think of very many more productive uses for your time than being outside in the sunshine and growing healthy vegetables for your family.

 ## Hobbies That Bless Others

Use your gifts to bless others. Here are some great gift ideas you can create with your hobbies:

❖ Faithbooking takes scrapbooking to a whole new level, creating a treasured heirloom to pass on to your children. There are lots of new resources developing. Type in "faithbooking" on your search engine to see samples and learn more. Here are a few good Web sites I've discovered:

www.remindersoffaith.com

www.walkingwithwisdom.com

www.scrapbookersbubblebath.com

www.bellaonline.com

❖ Make homemade cards and then send a note to someone just to tell them you love them and how much you appreciate them. The time and care that went into making the card will also reflect your words.

❖ Create gifts for birthdays, holidays, anniversaries, and other gift-giving occasions. There are lots of great books with homemade craft ideas, including Karen Ehman's *Homespun Gifts from the Heart.*[15]

Hobby Ideas on a Budget

Several of the crafts our moms and grandmothers did all the time give hours of enjoyment at very little relative cost.

❖ Consider crochet, knitting, or needlepoint. The initial investment is minimal and, because of the intricacies, you can spend hours creating something that can be kept as a treasured heirloom.

❖ Sewing is also a great hobby when you're on a budget, because the items you create are very useful, whether it's clothes, curtains, pillows, tablecloths, or entire room ensembles. Sewing classes are readily available, and a repair shop is a great place to pick up a used machine for a small investment.

❖ Garage sales are a great hobby, especially for women who need their "shopping urge" scratched! Who wouldn't like to find a Barbie dollhouse, complete with all the furniture, in mint condition for fifteen dollars at a neighbor's house? And what a great way to teach your children about being good stewards.

Not All Hobbies Require a Glue Gun!

❖ Write poetry, short stories, children's stories, an autobiography, or biographies of your family.

❖ Create a family tree and discover your genealogy.

❖ Take up painting or another classic art form. Donna Dewberry has a great technique you can learn: "One Stroke" painting (www.onestroke.com). You can create beautiful items and artwork with this method.

❖ Take music lessons. You are never too old to learn something new.

❖ One of the ladies in my MomTime group gave herself a special graduation present: she tried out and landed the lead in a local theater production of *Shadowlands.* It was a great production and a super experience for her.

Don't already have a hobby? Learn one. Many hobby stores and craft shops offer classes. Community colleges also offer many creative classes. Do any of these tickle your fancy?

❖ Art Classes

❖ Jewelry Making

❖ Floral Arranging

❖ Piano Lessons

❖ Photography

❖ Calligraphy

❖ Ballroom Dancing

❖ Pottery

❖ Gift Wrapping

❖ Decoupage

❖ Rubber Stamping

❖ Faux Finish Painting

❖ Stained Glass

❖ Mosaics

❖ Knitting. Not only is it easy to take your knitting with you anywhere, but you can knit on a budget and make gifts for other people. No wonder it is God's personal hobby.

For you formed my inward parts;
you knitted me together in my mother's womb.
Psalm 139:13

If you are still reading this book, then you may be ready to turn the page and read my next wild and crazy theory: I think God likes to see us having fun. There, I've said it. No, I didn't say He likes to see us full of joy. That would be too easy; we know that to be true. Think about it. Laughter is a big deal in our lives and God created it. We can be full of joy and not laugh. But it is less likely that we will laugh unless we are having fun. Are you following my logic? Stick with me here and see if I can convince you.

14

Fun

Good Medicine

When I left show business behind to concentrate on being a full-time wife and mother, I was thrilled. I loved every minute of staying home with my kids. But even as much as I enjoyed the luxury of being a stay-at-home mom, there were times I felt isolated and alone. The alternative—getting all three toddlers ready and taking them out in public somewhere—was even less inviting.

One day I was feeling especially desperate for some adult conversation, so I called up a couple of friends and invited them over for lunch on Friday. They brought their little ones over, and we put them all down for naps. Then we ate lunch and played games for two hours. We laughed like we hadn't laughed in years. It was the kind of laugh where you know what you're laughing about really isn't that funny, but you so desperately need to laugh that it doesn't matter. When you finally regain some composure, your sides are aching, your pants are wet (childbirth, you know), and you feel as refreshed as if you had just had a good cry—only better, because you're not sad!

My friends and I decided that we needed this more often. We felt so rejuvenated! One of the other moms offered to cook, and we set a date for the following Friday. That was over a dozen years ago and the beginning of MomTime. Back then I called my weekly moms' group "The Good Medicine Club," referring to Proverbs 17:22—"A joyful heart is good medicine"—because we laughed so much and felt so good afterward.

One of the reasons we looked forward to each week was because we took turns cooking something special. You know, girl food. First off, it was just nice to be eating something other than Beanie Weenies or leftover chicken nuggets or the cut-off crusts from a peanut butter and jelly sandwich. We each tried recipes that we knew our husbands would complain about and our children would hold their noses while eating the requisite number of bites. It was also a treat just to have someone else do the cooking and serve us.

Hands down, my favorite part of our time together was the games! I *love* playing games. I have a whole closet full, so we played a different game each week. It is surprising what you can learn about people when you compete with them. Their real personality comes out, and it is often hysterical. There were days we couldn't even see the dots on the dice because of the tears of laughter streaming down our faces. We had so much fun, and we counted down the days until we would laugh that hard again the next week.

Psalm 16:11 says, "You will show me the path of life; in Your presence is fullness of joy; at Your right hand are pleasures forevermore" (NKJV). Psalm 27:6 says, "And now my head shall be lifted up above my enemies all around me; therefore I will offer sacrifices of joy in His tabernacle; I will sing, yes, I will sing praises to the LORD" (NKJV).

Revelation 4:11 says we were created for God's pleasure. We read in the verses above that at His right hand are pleasures forevermore and in His presence is fullness of joy. God even receives our joy as a form of worship. He created us with the capacity for joy and pleasure and laughter and fun. He doesn't begrudge us good, clean fun. I believe He loves to see us enjoying ourselves and the gift of life He's given us. I think it brings Him joy.

Of course, we must use wisdom. Proverbs 21:17 says, "He who loves pleasure will be a poor man; he who loves wine and oil will not be rich" (NKJV). Something tells me that most moms reading this book aren't struggling with the fact that they're having too much fun. Our dilemma is trying to find time for a bit of refreshing laughter.

Learning the importance of having fun is good for us emotionally and physically. Scientific studies have shown laughter to reduce blood pressure, strengthen the immune system by restricting stress hormones, and it is an aerobic workout for the heart and lungs!

Laughter is not only good for you, it is also good for your families. (I realize, even after reading this far into the book, I still need to convince you that wanting to have fun is not selfish; ultimately, it is going to serve your family as much as it does you.)

Moms set the tone in the home. If we know how to have fun, then we will create an atmosphere that is lighthearted and full of healthy laughter. We can turn tense situations into opportunities for mercy by making a joke rather than an issue out of mistakes. We will be quicker to laugh over spilled milk than cry over it.

I've even discovered ways to make discipline fun. Who said correction has to be boring to be effective?! We need to have more fun with our kids. It is good for them and even better for us. Too often, in the busyness and pressure of raising kids, we lose perspective of the privilege of being a mother. Having fun reminds us that we really do enjoy these little troublemakers!

Join me in the next Rest Stop, and let's see if we can have a little fun.

ℱun—ℛest Stop
ℱun at ℋome—ℐt's ℱundamental

A merry heart does good, like medicine,
but a broken spirit dries the bones.
Proverbs 17:22 NKJV

Laughter is good for the heart. It is good for the body. It is also "fun-da-mental!" Having fun with your husband and kids can establish memories you'll never forget. Here are some of my favorite ideas for creating fun at home with little or no cost:

 Creativity

Be creative! Turn your home into a fun play land with these simple ideas:

❖ Build a puppet stage with chairs and sheets; write a story and perform for Dad when he gets home.

❖ Put up the camping tent in the living room for a safari adventure
   (or build one with chairs and sheets).

❖ Horsey rides

❖ Tickle torture

❖ Pillow fights

❖ Rent a classic comedy. (Carol Burnett, Don Knotts, and *I Love Lucy* are lots of fun to watch!)

❖ Puzzles are great too. Consider a portable table where the puzzle can stay out until it is finished. This allows you to work on it over several days.

❖ Create instruments from objects around the house and march all around like a marching band.

❖ Have a paper airplane distance contest.

❖ Play with your kids! Buy some play-doh, coloring books, Lite Brite® or an Easy Bake® oven and relive your childhood with your kids. Don't just teach and train them; get down on the floor with them and play dolls, Barbies,® Hot Wheels®, blocks, LEGOs®, or anything else that's fun.

Board Games

If your husband enjoys games, make a particular night "game night" when the meal is simple and the only activity after dinner is games. This is infinitely better than watching TV. My children love these games:

❖ Cranium®

❖ Cadoo®

❖ Dominoes®

❖ Chicken Foot®

❖ Scene-It Disney Edition®

I occasionally host a game night at our home, and even people who swear they don't like games enjoy it. And those of us who are "game fanatics" have tons of fun trouncing our opponents! Try one of these games:

- ❖ Catch Phrase®
- ❖ Guesstures®
- ❖ Taboo®
- ❖ Bingo®
- ❖ Bunko®
- ❖ Double Nine Dominos®

 **Mealtime Fun**

Make mealtimes fun! Here are a few easy ideas:

- ❖ Make Mickey-Mouse–eared or chocolate chip pancakes.
- ❖ Have a cookie decorating contests for dessert.
- ❖ Make ice cream sundaes with sauces, sprinkles, and whipped cream.
- ❖ Go to a party store, buy paper goods and decorations off the clearance table, and celebrate whatever season was on sale in the middle of the year.
- ❖ Let the kids be restaurant servers.
- ❖ Make a house out of cardboard boxes and eat in it.

* Buy a cake at the grocery store and have them write "Happy Monday" on it. Celebrate after dinner for no particular reason.

* Have each family member choose a crazy utensil from your gadget drawer and eat your meal with this instead of a fork or spoon. For example, eat soup with a pasta server, macaroni and cheese with a pie server, etc.

 **Fun in the Car**

Play games in the car. Here are some games you can play with the entire family:

* Sing old favorites: "On Top of Spaghetti," "Found a Peanut," "The Ants Came Marching One-by-One."

* Pray for the food and the family behind you in the fast-food lane.

* Pay the toll booth for the car behind you.

* Play "Twenty Questions."

 **Outdoor Fun**

Kids need physical activity and physical love—make sure they get a daily dose of something you are both involved in:

* Tag

* Hide-and-Seek

* Dodgeball

* Croquet

* Basketball

❖ water balloon fight

❖ Treasure hunt with clues and prizes

❖ Flashlight tag

 **Fun for Free!**

Take advantage of free entertainment:

❖ Parks

❖ Playgrounds

❖ Libraries

❖ Community centers

❖ YMCA/YWCA

❖ Malls

❖ Museums that have a free day or afternoon

 Take a Hometown Family Vacation

Plan a "hometown" family vacation—do all the fun things you usually don't get to do in your community:

❖ Putt-Putt golf

❖ Go-cart track

❖ Go for an ice-cream cone or sno-cone

❖ Zoo

❖ Local theme parks

❖ Special restaurants

❖ Movies

❖ One night at a hotel with pool

❖ Bowling

❖ Arcades

❖ Tour the fire station and slide down the pole

Do Something Zany

❖ Show up at your husband's workplace with the kids and a picnic.

❖ Next time you are sitting in the drive-thru of a fast-food restaurant, order in a silly voice or funny accent. When you pull up to the pick-up window, act normal. (My kids used to love this.)

❖ Set up a lemonade stand with your children.

❖ "Kidnap" your children from their beds and take them out to breakfast in their pajamas.

❖ Throw a party for all of the neighborhood dogs. Serve dog treats and play party games with the pets and their owners.

❖ One afternoon, load the kids up in the car and stop and ask people for directions. (I mean ask them which way they think you should go and turn that way. See where you end up.)

About this time you may be thinking, *All she ever does is read, scrapbook, play games and do crazy things.* You know, that is not true. If that were the case, I would be upstairs right now with my daughters playing pool. I have to find some time to work in between all this fun I'm having.

People ask me all the time how I'm able to juggle so many balls: homeschooler, wife, author, speaker, scrapbooker, etc. I usually tell them that the way I do it is by knowing I'm going to drop a few balls now and then. I'm really not that good of a juggler. At any given time, some ball, somewhere, is coming crashing down to the ground before I can catch it.

There are many other answers to this question: my kids are older, my husband works at home, my mom lives nearby, I never sleep (just kidding). There is also one more reason. I'm manic about organization. Turn the page and you'll see what I'm talking about.

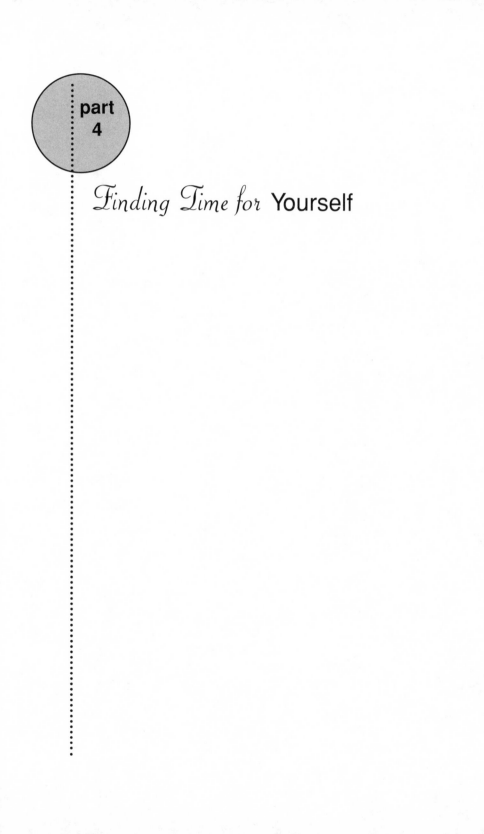

**part
4**

Finding Time for Yourself

15

Organization

They Call Me "Obsessive-Compulsive Miss Order"

They say a picture is worth a thousand words, so rather than share a handful of stories about why I think organization is so crucial to success in motherhood, I'm going to show you a few of the charts and lists I've created over the last dozen years or so. Hopefully they will spark your own ideas about how to adapt them to your unique family.

I've also uploaded the templates of these charts and lists to my Web site. If you are interested in downloading them for your personal use, feel free to surf over to www.LisaWhelchel.com and look in the "Me in Mommy" section.

My all-time favorite list ever created was a gift to me for Mother's Day many, many years ago. My husband, who is a computer whiz, noticed that each and every morning I drew two vertical lines on a legal pad and labeled each of the three columns, "Phone," "Do," and "Go." Each day, before the kids woke up, I would transfer any remaining tasks that had not been crossed off the day before onto a fresh to-do list.

Needless to say, this was a lot of redundant work, because I never actually completed even half of the tasks on my list in one day. The following chart is the thoughtful gift my husband created for me. This chart is so simple, but I go back to it time and time again.

Lisa's Organizer

✓	Phone	✓	Do	✓	Go

Steve was so pleased with how well I received his gift that he offered to create a grocery store chart for me the following Mother's Day. The two of us took a trip (probably a date-night outing) to the grocery store where I did most of my shopping. We started on the left side of the store near the bakery department and made our way up and down each aisle until we ended up on the other side of the store in produce, making notes about what was on each aisle and along the perimeter.

The result was the following chart:

Bread	Deli	Dairy	Frozen	Cleaning	Toiletries	Meat

Snacks	Cereal	Drinks	Baking	Canned	Pasta	Produce

Every week, all I had to do was print out one of these charts and hang it on the side of the fridge. Whenever I noticed we needed to buy something at the store, I filled that item in the appropriate column. Then, when I headed to the grocery store, all I had to do was start on the left and end up on the right without any retracing of my steps! Talk about a time saver and stress reducer.

I've tried many things over the years to make cooking healthy meals for my family more of a privilege than a chore. Perhaps the most beneficial tip

I've discovered is to set aside a few hours to plan your meals for the week, write out your grocery list, and do your shopping all at once. Then you don't have to worry about looking at an empty pantry at four o'clock one afternoon wondering how you can whip up something yummy with a can of tuna and some flour tortillas. The following chart is an example of one month's meal calendar. (The letters and numbers represent the cookbooks and page number.)

Cauble Family Menu

Mon.	Tues.	Wed.	Thurs.	Fri.	Sat.	Sun.	Breakfasts	Steve's Lunch
AWANA/ Date Nite	FF-165 Italian Vege Pasta Noodles Garlic Bread	Choir Kids' Leftovers	Chicken Rice Vegetable Rolls	Leftovers from MomTime	BCC-146 Michele's BBQ Ribs	BCC-181 Turkey/Rice Cass. BCC-99 Cheesy Corn	Cereal Pop Tarts Smoothies Pillsbury Rolls Cherry/Angel Food Trifle Wheat Rolls	Leftovers Deli Meat Sandwich PB & Banana Sandwiches
Mon.	Tues.	Wed.	Thurs.	Fri.	Sat.	Sun.	Kids' lunch	Snacks
AWANA/ Date Nite	Cream of Broccoli & Cheese Soup Muffins	Choir Fast Food	CP-84 Lazy Day Stew Yeast Rolls	Leftovers from MomTime	Pizza Family Night	Grandma's House	Beanies C. Nuggets Fish Stix PB & J Deli S. wich Leftovers	Apple Slices Frozen Fruit Beef Jerky Apple Sauce Celery & PB Carrots & Ranch
Mon.	Tues.	Wed.	Thurs.	Fri.	Sat.	Sun.	Rush Dinners	Cookbooks
AWANA/ Date nite	DH-121 Beef Stroganoff Steamed Broccoli Rolls	Choir Kids' Leftovers	Party	Leftovers from MomTime	DH-62 Oriental Salad Frozen Egg Rolls	Cafeteria	TV Dinners Reheat Pizza Cereal Grilled Cheese Chicken Salad	MM=Make A Mix C=Cauble Book CP= Pr. Cooker PC= Pr. Cooker DH= Deep in Heart BCC= Best of .Cook H=Holland Grill
Mon.	Tues.	Wed.	Thurs.	Fri.	Sat.	Sun.		
AWANA/ Date nite	DH-39 Easy Chili Cornbread	Choir Fast Food	FF-63 German Potato Soup Cheese Rolls	Leftovers from MomTime	Pizza Family Night	CC-19 Pork Chops & Gravy CC-94 Baked Apples		

I wish I had kept some of the many chore charts and lists I created for my children when they were really little. I even had my stepdad, Roy, draw little pictures of toothbrushes, baths, and Bibles, because they were too young to read but old enough to begin making good habits.

Here is a chore chart from a few years ago:

Cauble Cid's Chore Chart

	✓ Clancy	✓ Tucker	✓ Haven
Mon.	Clean Kids' Bathroom Bring Dumpsters in To Gate Dump Recycle Wipe Counters & Table after eating	Get Mail Dump Little Trashes Load & Unload Dishwasher Take Kitchen Trash Out	Declutter House Sweep & Scrub Floor Clear Coffee Table
Tues.	Declutter House Bring Glasses Down from Upstairs	Sweep and scrub Floor Clean Kids' Bathroom Wipe Counter & Kitchen table all day	Get Mail Load & Unload Dishwasher Clear Coffee Table
Wed.	Get Mail Load & Unload Dishwasher Clear Coffee Table	Declutter House Sweep and Scrub Floor Wipe Counters & Table All Day	Clean Kids' bathroom Refresh Toilet Paper
Thurs.	Switch Laundry Declutter House Sweep & Scrub Floor	Sort Laundry Clean Kids' Bathroom Wipe Counters & Table All Day	Dump Hampers Load & Unload Dishwasher Get Mail
Fri.	Clean backyard Wipe Counters & Table All Day	Clean out Van Load and unload Dishwasher	Spring Clean Room & Closet Get Mail
Sat.	Get Mail Load & Unload Dishwasher Write Thank You Note	Declutter House Wipe Counters & Table All Day	Write Thank You Note Clean Kids' bathroom Sweep & Scrub Floor
Sun.	Cooking Day	Take Dumpsters to the Street—PM	Cooking Day

We don't give our kids an allowance, and we don't pay for chores. Instead, we've tried to emphasize that helping around the house is a way for them to serve the family. However, we do give "bonuses" for diligence and initiative. If they are able to complete their responsibilities excellently without being reminded, then they receive a checkmark at the end of the day.

We also give them opportunities to earn bonus money for a specific task, depending on which area we are working on for each child. (There is also a debit column for "creative correction" purposes.)

On Saturday evenings, we tally up their points and pay a nickel for each mark and extra for special incentive chores. Then we figure savings and tithe for the next morning. The chart on the facing pages shows what their responsibility charts look like at this season of our children's lives:

I also have a chart for privileges/conditions and house rules/consequences. I'll upload those templates to the Web site.

You've already witnessed enough of my crazed organizer tendencies. (By this time you're thinking I probably have "spontaneous sex" scheduled in my PalmPilot.) To seal the fate on my hyperscheduling disposition, I'm going to share one last chart. This is only one sample of dozens of family schedules I've created over the years: (I'll upload a few more generic charts and samples on my Web site, for families who don't homeschool, single parents, and dads who work later in the evening.)

Please remember that I never actually follow any of these charts, schedules, or lists completely on any given day. They are simply guidelines that I attempt to live by. There has to be plenty of flex room, or I would drive myself and my family completely insane.

I can hear some of you saying, "If flexibility is the key and things get changed around, then why have a detailed plan?" Perhaps some of this is just personality and preferences. Every mom reading this book needs to find what works for her.

For me, if I don't have a plan, then my priorities don't get done and my goals go unrealized. Life runs me rather than my ordering my days to match what I believe God has instructed me to do.

Obviously, balance is the key. You may be the type of person who looks at all these charts and thinks, *Why create all that paperwork? Just go with the flow and take the day as it comes.* I gotta hand it to you, there is certainly a time and a place for that kind of attitude. Honestly, as moms, if we can't

WORK CHART FOR THE WEEK OF

EVERYDAY TASKS	Mon.	Tue.	Wed.	Thurs.	Fri.	Sat.	Sun.
Get Up On Time (7:00 a.m. school days 8:00 a.m. weekends)						X	X
Make Bed							
Daily Chore							
Take Vitamins							
Completed School Work							
Practice Instrument (30 Mins.)							
Clean Room & Bathroom							
Read Bible, Devotional & Pray							
Lights Out On Time (10:00 school nights; midnight weekends)							
Assigned Books Completed							
JOBS	Mon.	Tue.	Wed.	Thurs.	Fri.	Sat.	Sun.
Clancy—Brush Donut							
Clancy—Walk Donut							
Clancy—Feed & Water Donut							
Tucker—Tests-A's							
Tucker—Tests—B's							
Tucker—Tests—C's							
Haven—Pull Orders & Ship Books							
Haven—Read & Complete Book for Pleasure							
Haven—Pick Up After Self							
DEBITS	Mon.	Tue.	Wed.	Thurs.	Fri.	Sat.	Sun.

taking care of the "me" in mommy

CAUBLE FAMILY SCHOOL SCHEDULE

	Tucker	Haven	Clancy	Mommy
7 :00	Wake & Read Bible	Wake & Read Bible	Wake & Read Bible	Devotions
:30	Bed, Dress & Teeth	Bed, Dress & Teeth	Bed, Dress & Teeth	Fix Breakfast
8 :00	Breakfast	Breakfast	Breakfast	Breakfast
:30	Chores	Kindergarten	Room Time	Teach Haven
9 :00	Free Time	Workbooks	Workbooks	Shower & Dress
:30	Workbooks	Room Time	Computer	Worship
10 :00	Piano Practice	Computer	Preschool	Teach Clancy
:30	Bible	Bible	Bible	Bible
11 :00	Math & Snack	Outside & Snack	Outside & Snack	Teach Tucker
:30	Outside Time	Outside Time	Outside Time	Fix Lunch
12 :00	Lunch	Lunch	Lunch	Lunch
:30	Sing, Spell, R & R	Nap	Nap	Teach Tucker
1 :00	Read Books	Read Books	Read Books	Teach Tucker
:30	Rest	Rest	Rest	My Work
2 :00	Rest	Rest	Rest	My Work
:30	Story Time	Story Time	Story Time	Story Time
3 :00	Music, snack & quiet	Music, snack & quiet	Music, snack & quiet	Prepare School
:30	School time	School time	School time	School time
4 :00	Outside time	Outside time	Outside time	Begin Dinner
:30	Outside time	Outside time	Outside time	Begin Dinner
5 :00	Clean Backyard	Pick up toys & room	Pick up toys & room	Freshen house & face
:30	Dinner	Dinner	Dinner	Dinner
6 :00	Shower/brush teeth	Bath/brush teeth	Bath/brush teeth	Clean Kitchen
:30	Daddy's book	Daddy's book	Daddy's book	Layout clothes & dinner
7 :00	Free time	Bedtime/Prayers	Bedtime/Prayers	Put girls to bed
:30				Prepare tomorrow's school work
8 :00				
:30	Bed Time			

chuck our schedule and follow the Spirit, or our toddler or husband or whatever is more *important* than *urgent*, then we set ourselves up for some serious frustration.

Even so, I think it is wise to start with a plan. First Corinthians 14 says, "God is not the author of confusion, but of peace," and a few verses down, "Let all things be done decently and in order" (vv. 33, 40 NKJV). We only have to look to the heavens to see the orderliness of God reflected in His handiwork.

I realize that many of you may be protesting, "But organization just isn't my thing!" I think this might be the biggest obstacle to creating a more orderly structure.

Maybe some people are born with an organizational gene—there certainly are people who enjoy and are extremely good at organization. But I also have seen firsthand that living out an organized life is definitely a learned skill.

There are lots of resources available—books, tapes, systems, seminars—to help you learn the art of better organization. Even entire TV shows these days are devoted to subjects of how to get organized.

So why is this also important for us as moms? The Bible tells us that the wisest man who ever lived, King Solomon, felt it was important to order his day. "Now all the work of Solomon was *well-ordered* from the day of the foundation of the house of the LORD until it was finished. So the house of the LORD was completed" (2 Chronicles 8:16 NKJV; emphasis added). We might want to take our cues from Solomon if we want our own "house of the Lord" completed.

Becoming organized might seem like a lot of work at first, but in the end, you'll save so much time and be much less stressed if you have some kind of daily schedule or routine. And, moms, what are you going to do with all this time you're going to save? Come on, now, you know the answer. You are going to do something for yourself!

You've already done something for your family, because by organizing even one area of your life, you will be less harried and you will be a more peaceful mommy. Just think of what a relaxed mommy you will be if you take that new "found" time in your day to refresh yourself in some way.

In addition to some of these ideas I've already shared, I've also included many more practical tips to organize your busy life and accomplish what you've set out to do in your heart in the Rest Stop that follows.

Organization—Rest Stop
Chart Your Course

I have friends who accuse me of being a micromanager when it comes to organizing my family life. I have no idea what they are talking about! Your temperament, on the other hand, may concur with this philosophy: *Organized people are just too lazy to look for things!* If so, then this will be a great Rest Stop for you.

 ## Calendar

Having a calendar to look at just before the beginning of the new month with *everything* that involves any of your time noted on it is a great starting place. From that "planning session," you can make lists of everything you need to do to make all of those things flow together well.

Here's a checklist for your planning session to make sure you get everything on next month's calendar. You should use this as your starting point and then make your own checklist that includes all the unique factors of your household:

❖ Enter all your church activities.

❖ Enter all your and your husband's activities.

❖ Enter all the kids' activities on the calendar.

❖ Look over your established list of priorities and goals, and check it against how the calendar is shaping up. For instance, are you having people over to your house too often, or not often enough? Are the kids getting overloaded with activities at the expense of their schoolwork? Are there conflicting activities with midterm test weeks? Do you and your husband have enough "alone" time on the calendar?

❖ Actively look for ways you can consolidate and simplify!

❖ Make a master list of all the items that need action. These would include:

- All instances where you and your husband will both be needed to take kids to activities in different directions

- All the times you're going to need sitters

- A list of anything that won't work so you can talk it through and make decisions about priorities or work out compromises

- Gifts you need to purchase

- Phone calls you need to make

- Other items you need to search for and acquire (hobby supplies; grocery items for a party, meal, or get-together)

Try to have all of these issues settled around the first of each month so everything is laid out and you can "post" the final calendar for the family to use. Of course, it never flows perfectly, so I do weekly reviews to make adjustments. Things get taken off, added, or moved around. Flexibility has to be key, or else you will feel like (and perhaps be) a drill sergeant instead of a mom!

❖ I prefer using Microsoft Outlook on my computer, because there are so many things that happen annually that can be automatically added to next year's calendar. I never have to re-record birthdays on my yearly calendar. In a click of the mouse, they are put into the next year's schedule.

 **Plan Ahead**

❖ Keep bags handy and already stocked with essentials for places you frequent. For instance you may prepare a few specific bags that contain some of the following items:

- **The pool**—swimsuits, towels, sunscreen, book to read, sunglasses, pool and sand toys, hat, change of clothes for kids, goggles, water wings, pool diapers, etc.

- **Grandma's house**—change of clothes, mini-diaper bag, snacks, medical release and insurance information, extra blankie or pacifier, toys

- **Church**—children's Bible, change for the offering, coloring book

- **Restaurant**—tiny toys, Gameboy, crayons, game books, stickers, bib, change of clothes, crackers or cheerios

- **Car rides**—pillow, book, music tapes, toys, games

❖ Purchase gifts when you see them (especially when on sale), and have a shelf or bin where they can be easily accessed. Then, when you have a children's birthday party or need a hostess gift when going over to someone's house for dinner, you have one without having to make a trip to the store.

❖ Keep a variety of greeting cards as well, so you always have one appropriate for the occasion. You can buy a whole box of cards for every occasion at card stores and online Web sites. I've found a great selection at www.currentcatalog.com.

 **Lists**

Keep a handful of lists going at all times. The moment you think of something, write it down. (Remember the placenta problem.) It is also important to have a specific place to store these lists so you always know where they can be found. For instance, magnetic lists on the fridge, drawer in the kitchen, by the computer, etc. Resist the temptation to remove the list from this spot or you may end up wasting time looking for this list that is supposed to help you save time. Here are a few ideas for lists you may want to make:

❖ Grocery

❖ Returns

❖ Phone calls

❖ Errands

❖ "Honey-do's"

❖ Things you're saving for

❖ Prayer requests

❖ Thank you notes

Group Like Things Together

Another way to think about organization is "grouping like things together." This can be anything from getting all the green beans on the same shelf to cleaning out the entire garage. But at its most basic point, organizing things is putting like things together for greater efficiency in finding and using those items. So here's a list to get you started thinking about "like things":

❖ Group your errands together. Take an afternoon and go to the grocery store, the cleaners, the car wash, the secondhand clothes shop, etc. This saves not only time but gas! Be sure to make a list, in order of your stops, before you head out. This will keep you from missing anything and having to backtrack. Remember, it takes less time (and gas) to do research by phone or Internet rather than going from one store to another looking for certain items.

❖ Group tasks together. For example, iron outfits for two days instead of just one. You'll end up saving time. Clean all the hard surface floors at once, rather than doing them one at a time. You'll save time filling buckets and collecting other supplies.

File It

At the beginning of each year, buy a cardboard file box and update the following files or customize this list for your family's needs:

❖ Insurance—Life

❖ Insurance—Property

❖ Insurance—Medical

❖ Add to Address Book

❖ School

❖ Immunizations

❖ Pet Info

❖ Warranties

❖ Important Papers—Birth Certificates, Dedication Certificates, Social Security #, etc.

❖ "Special" Items—i.e., e-mail encouragement note

 ## Favorite Organizing Resources and Tips

❖ Seriously consider purchasing a PDA, Personal Digital Assistant, such as a PalmPilot or Pocket PC. You can often find great deals on last year's model or on an online auction site. These handy-dandy tools will keep your calendar, contacts, lists, notes, files, and just about everything else organized in the palm of your hand.

❖ Hang whole outfits on a hanger for your children the night before.

❖ Buy a magnetic note pad and stick it on the refrigerator. As soon as you run out of an item, immediately add it to the list. Teach your children to do the same thing.

❖ Keep a small notebook with a pen attached in your purse, near your computer, or in the kitchen—anywhere handy so you can jot down things you need to remember later. This not only keeps you organized but also allows you to stay on task, rather than attempting to do something before you forget it.

❖ Take pictures of or scan your children's art and school work. This relieves guilt for not keeping everything and keeps your house from getting too cluttered. Rather than throw away these "treasures" send them to relatives, soldiers, or nursing homes with a handwritten note from your child. (The more primary the spelling and printing the better!)

 ## Simplify

One of the greatest obstacles to organization is too much stuff! As often as possible, delete it, purge it, give it away, sell it, toss it, or just say no.

❖ Look at your schedule and pick one thing to give up.

❖ Purge closets often, including the pantry. Teach kids to give to the needy by delivering items to shelters or thrift stores.

❖ Sort through one drawer a day. (Maybe take two days for the "junk drawer.")

❖ Purchase clear, medium-sized containers and label them with each child's name. When something is too sentimental to throw away, but too much "clutter" to keep around, put it in your child's "Special Box" to send off with them after they leave home.

❖ Don't hang on to mail or other papers you don't really need. Try to make a decision about the paper when you're handling it for the first time. Put that bill directly into the bill sorter; put that insurance policy directly into the permanent file. If you know you probably won't make it to the grocery store by the time the sale ad runs out, toss it immediately. This prevents you from handling those papers twice and the pileup that inevitably results from collecting things to deal with them later.

A Word about Computers

It is pretty obvious by now how much I rely on my computer and other technology tools. Especially when it comes to organization, I love to live on the cutting edge. (Must be that one-flesh thing with my adorable computer geek husband.)

While the computer can be a great tool for so many things, don't let it consume too much of your time. Budget and plan your time and computer activities so precious hours don't get "sucked" into the computer vacuum.

I'm definitely a huge fan of the computer and it makes my life infinitely simpler, but like most things, there can be too much of a good thing. Our pastor, Ed Young Jr., encourages us to periodically take a Sabbath from technology. This is harder than you might imagine, but it gives you the opportunity to get back in touch with things that technology hinders: communication, vulnerability, one-on-one time with each other rather than a machine, and so on.

When my children were younger, I spent a lot of time online buying and selling used homeschool curriculum. One day I came to the realization that I was saving money, but losing time. I determined that my time taking care of my family and home was ultimately more valuable, so I chose to stop spending so much time on the computer so I could invest that time more wisely.

There is something about spending too much time on the computer that will drag you down. If you find yourself guilty of this, set a timer for fifteen minutes. When the timer sounds, get up and don't return for a few more hours.

If you are truly addicted, either because of spending too much time, or too much money shopping online, or chatting with friends instead of your family, or going to places that are not healthy for you emotionally or spiritually, then pluck it out! Unplug it and put it away for a season. In the meantime, come up with a plan for controlling your computer rather than it controlling you.

Whether it is the computer, television, radio, or any other form of technology, if the enemy is able to use it to further his plans in your life, family, or home, then take control and throw it out. Yes, you will have to give up the good with the bad, but in your more rational moments, you know it is the right thing to do.

Takin' It to the Next Level

Now, if this little Rest Stop on organization has gotten you excited about decluttering, reordering, labeling, and simplifying, then you may want to buy a whole book about it. There are so many incredible resources available to help order your world so you can provide your family with a less stressful, more peaceful home environment. Here are a few of the books I recommend:

❖ *The Family Manager Takes Charge* by Kathy Peel

❖ *More Hours in My Day* by Emilie Barnes

❖ *The Messies Manual* by Sandra Felton

❖ *How to Organize (Just About) Anything* by Peter Walsh

We are about to enter uncharted territory. Not that I haven't created a chart or two for housekeeping, cooking, and finances, I have. I'm just not very good at following them. Before we head into these next three chapters, let me just tell you up front. I don't know where we're going or how to get there. I'm not a very good housekeeper (Steve is better than I am). I'm an awful cook. (When I cook, I usually burn everything.) And I stink with money. (We have almost been in bankruptcy court twice.)

Maybe this confession, more than my perfection, gives me authority to write the next chapter on housekeeping. I need help. If you do too, then join me and we'll find it together.

16

Housekeeping

Let the Dust Settle

I keep a Mason jar full of rocks, pebbles, and sand on the shelf above my computer to remind me of how I want to spend my time. Let me share the story. Many years ago, my kids and I created this jar as a homeschool assignment. (You know us home-schoolers: we can turn a walk to the mailbox into a field trip.)

We bought a bag of rocks, pebbles, and sand from the local Hobby Lobby®. (It is really difficult to go on a nature walk in the middle of Los Angeles, but we *were* able to squeeze in a short science lesson in the silk flower aisle.)

When we got home, I asked the kids to pour the sand into the jar; then add the pebbles; and, finally, add the bigger rocks. As you probably guessed, the jar was too full to fit any of the rocks into it. So I had them empty everything out and start over. This time I told them to put the rocks in first and then add the peb-bles. Finally, they poured the sand into the jar and watched as the tiny grains made their way into the empty spaces between the rocks and the pebbles. There was room for everything this time!

I explained that the rocks represent the different ways to feed our spirits and connect with God, the pebbles symbolize our relationships with other people, and the sand is a good illustration for the many other things in our lives, (especially dusting). If we make our to-do list, material things, or day-to-day *stuff* a priority, then we will barely have any time to spend with other people, and have even less room for God in our lives.

But if we make seeking God our first priority, perhaps through Bible study, prayer, and worship, and then make a conscious choice to put people above things, we will see that the other *stuff* that is legitimately important will ultimately be taken care of as well.

I have tried to live my life by this illustration, and, believe me, it takes an act of my will every single day. There are always so many pressing demands, urgent needs, deadlines, desires—all good things! And I want to do them all. But I've learned that if I do them all, or even attempt to, then my friends, family, and relationship with God always suffer.

Jesus explains this so much better than I ever could. Read how the Bible puts it:

> As Jesus and the disciples continued on their way to Jerusalem, they came to a village where a woman named Martha welcomed them into her home. Her sister, Mary, sat at the Lord's feet, listening to what he taught. But Martha was worrying over the big dinner she was preparing. She came to Jesus and said, "Lord, doesn't it seem unfair to you that my sister just sits here while I do all the work? Tell her to come and help me." But the Lord said to her, "My dear Martha, you are so upset over all these details! There is really only one thing worth being concerned about. Mary has discovered it—and I won't take it away from her." (Luke 10:38–42 NLT)

Let's say you have a choice to make between, say, doing the dishes, spending time with your child, or reading your Bible. How should you spend your time? My first question to you would be, "Have you spent any time strengthening your relationship with the Lord today?" If not, then on the grounds of Matthew 6:33—"But seek first the kingdom of God and his righteousness, and all these things will be added to you"—I'd have to recommend a bit of quiet time sitting at Jesus' feet.

Now, let's say you were able to get up a few minutes before the sun *or* son rose (whichever the case may be) to connect with your Best Friend in all the world (and beyond). Then I'd wholeheartedly recommend you let the dishes stay dirty a little while longer and go cuddle with your toddler or talk to your teenager. (Yes, I know that the dishes will be more difficult to clean the longer you wait.)

Proverbs 14:4 says, "Where there are no oxen, the manger is clean, but abundant crops come by the strength of the ox." My personal paraphrase of that scripture is, "If you didn't have any children, your house would stay cleaner. But there's so much more to life than a clean house—like the amazing blessing of family." Some days, let the dishes stack up and pull out a board game. Or forget vacuuming and go to the park instead. You may have to come home to a dirty house, but it's much better than coming home to an empty one.

I'm certainly not suggesting you never clean your house, pay the bills, or do the boring tasks of life. There are many other scriptures showing us the importance of diligence, responsibility, and hospitality. I'm simply reminding you to make a conscious choice either way.

Don't fall into bed at the end of the day and realize you really haven't accomplished anything. Your to-do list is still *to do*. You could have sworn you washed the dishes today, but it appears they need to be washed again. You put checks in the mail only to discover there were more bills already in the box waiting for you. And, worst of all, you can't remember one complete conversation you had with your children that didn't contain either a command or a reprimand.

I've discovered that a few simple housekeeping tips can make all the difference in the world. By implementing even a couple of the time-saving techniques I've included in the following Rest Stop, you will be amazed. You will have a cleaner house, which will make you feel better inside and out. You will save time with your daily housecleaning chores, which in turn means you can spend more time on yourself—enjoying your family. (See, I'm not completely self-centered. I understand that many times the best way to take care of ourselves is to simply have time to spend with our family.)

Read on, I've collected a bunch of ideas to help you take care of the housekeeping details and have plenty of time to take care of the little oxen— I mean children—too!

Housekeeping—Rest Stop
I'll Have a Maid in Heaven

For me, the key to housekeeping is to *break it up!* There will rarely be a time when your entire house is clean, top to bottom. That's unrealistic, so don't even allow yourself that expectation. Instead, try to organize your tasks and do part of the work every day. Consistency is the key to housekeeping not becoming overwhelming, because you can handle doing a few things each day and also because you'll actually be getting the housecleaning done. If you wait for the time when you can "really clean" or "clean it all at once," you may be waiting a long time!

 ## Quick Tips

My first tip is to send you directly to www.flylady.net. There is no need to reinvent the wheel, and this Web site has just about every tip you would ever need to get and keep your house in tip top shape. The Fly Lady is encouraging, relentless, forgiving, and practical. What a great combination. There are also tons of tips in the areas of finances, cooking, organization, and many other areas. Just in case you don't have access to the Internet at this very minute, or you're reading this book while taking a hot bath (hopefully), then I have listed a few helpful housekeeping ideas I've collected along the way:

❖ Clean the shower while taking a shower. Keep brush, squeegee, and cleaner in the shower for this purpose.

❖ Keep a spray bottle (¾ full of water with ¼ Pine-Sol) and paper towels under each bathroom sink. Have older boys spray and wipe around the bottom of toilet and bowl lip every day.

❖ Laundry baskets (and similar containers) are great tools for straightening. Use a basket for going from room to room and picking up everything that doesn't belong in that room. Then have a central point where you dump all of that stuff and sort everything into a different container for each room where the item belongs. Then you can take just that container to the correct room and empty.

Deeper Cleaning

❖ Go through each room with three garbage sacks: one for trash, one for giveaway, and one for items that need to be sorted and/or put back into place. When you're done with each room, you only have one bag to sort—the rest go away.

❖ Consider deep-cleaning one room each month (in addition to your routine housecleaning). This could be everything from ceiling fixtures to baseboards. It could include reorganizing closets, underbed storage containers, toy boxes, etc. Doing one room a month breaks these major tasks into bite-sized pieces.

❖ You can also create an annual schedule for tasks. Clean the light fixtures twice a year in April and October, clean out closets seasonally in May and November, clean the garage in February and August, and so on. By having a list and pattern, you can observe the garage clutter and not be so frustrated, knowing that twice a year, it's on your schedule of tasks.

❖ When your children are little, consider swapping out a Saturday morning and afternoon of child care with another family so you and Dad can clean out the garage or do a deep cleaning for the holidays or some other entertaining event. Not having the kids at the house will help you get more done and focus your activities.

❖ If at all possible, try to squeeze room in the budget to have a cleaning service come in to do heavy cleaning. (I once saw a book entitled, *A Housekeeper Is Cheaper than a Divorce.*) Twice a month works well and keeps you from getting overwhelmed or feeling like a constant "taskmaster" with your kids. Try to plan activities outside the house for housekeeping days to facilitate the service being as efficient as possible. Preparation and organization is the key to getting the most out of this service as well. Having detailed lists of what you want done and letting them spend their time really cleaning after you have straightened everything the day before gets the most benefit.

❖ Clutter is one of the biggest enemies of organization. Choose a room, make an appointment to tackle it and schedule it on the calendar, set an absolute deadline for completing the task, and designate a reward for thoroughly decluttering, cleaning, and organizing that room.

Favorite Laundry Tips

❖ Color-code all white socks (or other items) with a stroke of fabric paint on the bottom—one color for each household member. This makes sock sorting much easier!

❖ Use hooks for kids' stuff. Pajamas, towels, jeans, and other clothes can be hung and worn twice or more rather than being thrown into the basket or hamper after one use.

❖ Fold sheets and put them in the matching pillowcase. This saves room in the linen closet and makes it easier to grab everything you need in one spot.

❖ Put a retractable laundry line in each shower (like they often have in hotels) for swim suits, beach towels, and wet washcloths. Teach the kids to hang dry all their wet items before tossing them in the hamper.

❖ Wash delicates by themselves on the gentle cycle (in a mesh bag, if needed) rather than by hand. Use your short, presoak cycle for delicates, running it twice—once for washing and once for rinsing (instead of hand washing).

❖ Consider multiple hamper bag systems in each of the kids' rooms or in the laundry room so you can sort as things go into the laundry basket. Then you can combine all the darks from all the rooms once or twice a week for washing.

❖ Buy a laundry basket for each family member. When their clean clothes are folded, put them into their basket. Each person takes their basket to their room and puts away their clothes. Leave the basket in the room to fill with dirty clothes. When it is filled, have them bring it to the laundry room to be washed and start all over again.

❖ Most "air dry" or "lay flat" items can be dried for five to ten minutes on a low-heat dryer setting. Test for three minutes the first time, and be sure to set a timer! This not only makes the air-dry time much less and keeps most items from dripping, but it also helps them not be so wrinkled.

Training Our Children

❖ When your children are older, get them involved in housekeeping! By the time kids are ten, they can do laundry and tons of other household chores. The entire family lives in the house, so everyone should have assignments, according to their age and ability, to help the family keep the house tidy.

❖ Even when children are very little, they can learn to pick up toys, clothes, and other items. If they aren't old enough to put them away correctly yet, create a counter, table, or other collection point and teach them to put all of their items there.

❖ Set a week and inspect kids' bedrooms every day—like dorm inspection at summer camp. The grand prize for the most organized room could be something significant.

❖ Get kids in the habit of making their beds each morning when they are very young. Use sleeping bags or other easy linens when they are little so they can do it themselves.

❖ Leave items at the top or bottom of the stairs for the kids to tote as they go. Anything left after bedtime gets sent to "time-out" for a week.

❖ Consider creating a chart someplace in the house, perhaps the fridge or laundry room, where all assignments are outlined by day for each household member. Spend time teaching your children how to do the task, and make sure they are doing it correctly and well. Incentives are always better, but punishment may be needed at first. Taking away favorite activities is great because it teaches them that work is required before play is allowed. It's also a great way to teach team mentality. The family lives together in the house, so the entire family has to care for all the needs of the household as a team.

❖ As soon as you return from the grocery store and your children are helping you unload the car and put away the groceries, put them to work planning ahead. Have one child wash all the fruit. Have another child open the cookie and snack bags. Have them individually wrap a handful of them to put in their lunches. This makes lunch preparation easier in the morning, and it also assures that the snacks will be there for lunches and not eaten when friends come over as dinner spoilers.

I'm having a party at my house tonight for everyone who lives on my street. I've lived here two years and I barely know my neighbors. The Lord convicted me about this recently, so I decided to throw a party. (Not because the Lord corrected me, although that does prove He loves me [Proverbs 3:12], and that is worth celebrating.) No, I've invited these fifty-some-odd-people, (not that some of them are odd, although they might be; I haven't met all of them) to share the love of Jesus with them by opening my heart and home.

Our house is tidy, but not perfect. (We will be closing and locking the bedroom and laundry room doors.) Clancy and I baked some cookies, and I have some leftover pumpkin roll that my aunt Barbara made. Steve is going to pick up a cake from the store on his way home, and we'll probably open this nut/tray/snack thing we received in the mail last week.

Other than some coffee and cider, that is all I plan to serve. You may think I'm a horrible hostess, and I probably am, but I know myself too well. If I felt like I had to put on a show to impress somebody, I would never open my home because I will definitely not be impressing anyone with my cooking or housekeeping finesse.

You may be a wonderful cook and homemaker. Still, even you may pick up a tip or two in the next Rest Stop. If, on the other hand, you know you could use a tip or twenty, then follow me into the kitchen and we'll talk about cooking.

17

Cooking

Break Some Homemade Bread

A few years ago, when Tucker, Haven, and Clancy were much younger, I was filming an interview in our house for a Mother's Day special. The producer asked permission to record the kids, and they were more than thrilled to oblige. One of the questions the reporter asked was, "Is your mommy a good cook?" They all three answered affirmatively and enthusiastically. I was so proud.

Then they began to elaborate. Haven piped up first. "Oh, yes, my mommy makes the best Eggos you've ever tasted." Tucker echoed her approval with, "Sometimes she even cooks fish sticks. Those are my favorites." Clancy added sincerely, "But the best thing she cooks for us is peanut butter and jelly sandwiches!"

My secret was out for the whole world to know. I'm really not a very good cook. I don't enjoy cooking, I dread going to the grocery store, and I hate cleaning and cutting all of the fruits and vegetables. I would rather spend my time a hundred different ways than taking hours to prepare a meal that will be gobbled up in fifteen minutes, followed by another half hour of cleaning up.

But I love being a mother, and I know how important it is to sit around the table together as a family for dinner in the evenings. So I've tried many solutions for minimum cooking with maximum mealtime memories.

One of the best ideas I ever tried was once-a-month or freezer cooking. I would get up really early on a Saturday morning and plan out my meals for a month, doubling many menus and bulking up on cooked hamburger, marinated chicken, and pasta meals. After visiting the grocery store, health-food store, and warehouse store, I was ready to begin cooking. Steve usually took the kids somewhere out of my hair. Occasionally my mom would come over and help me cook, and then we would divvy up the meals.

I would look through my recipes and brown all of the hamburger, marinate all of the chicken, cook all of the sauces, clean and chop all of the vegetables—basically bunch as many activities together at one time as possible. Then it was time to assemble individual dinners in casserole dishes or Ziploc freezer bags. By the end of the day, my back was aching, my feet were killing me, and my hands were raw and pruny—but it was worth it because I didn't have to cook again for a whole month!

Steve would usually take us all out to dinner that night, because preparing supper was the last thing I wanted to do at that point. For the rest of the month, all I had to do was take out an entrée from the freezer the night before, put it in the fridge to thaw, and cook it the following evening with a side of vegetables and rolls and iced tea. The kids thought it was downright gourmet.

When I first moved to Texas a few years ago, one of the ways I was able to make some friends was by joining a dinner co-op. Once a month I would make eight dishes of one entrée. For instance, one month I cooked eight quiches, the next month I made eight bags of stir-fry, and one month I made eight pizza hoagies. (Don't ask.)

All of the other ladies in the group did the same thing. Then we would meet at somebody's house, have a brief time of fellowship, exchange our meals, and go home with eight different, delicious entrées. (Except for that one ridiculous pizza hoagie disaster.) This co-op was such a blessing for so many reasons. I made some new friends, and on seven nights of the month I didn't have to think about cooking. My whole family loved trying all the new dishes.

Over the years I've tried everything from fifteen-minute cooking to make-a-mix preparation to allergy-free recipes to low-carb, low-cal, low-fat, low-taste cooking and everything in between. Of course, the Crockpot and grill are timeless time savers.

My very favorite cooking experiment was "Sunday cooking with the girls." On Saturdays, Haven, Clancy, and I would sit around the table reading through my cookbooks. Each of us would choose one entrée and one dessert to prepare. We would make out our grocery list for these recipes and head out to the store.

Sunday afternoon, after our Sabbath nap ritual, the girls would meet in the kitchen to prepare our dishes together. I was there to supervise their work and teach them what little I knew about measuring, sifting, dicing, folding, browning, and making a big kitchen mess. By the end of the evening, we had a delicious meal prepared for that night and two more for Tuesday and Thursday nights—including dessert!

Recently, I discovered the luxury of make-ahead meals from various franchises. I've visited Dream Dinners®, Super Suppers®, and The Dinner Station®—and there are more of these incredible stores popping up every day. They are so popular because they are just what busy moms need.

Somebody else does the meal planning, grocery shopping, and cleaning and chopping. All you have to do is show up and put your meals together. As a matter of fact, I have a platter of seasoned fish thawing in the fridge right this minute. I sat out a box of rice just a minute ago. I put some bread mix in the bread machine this morning, and now all I have to do is steam some vegetables, cook the rice, and pop some Pillsbury rolls in the oven, and—voilà!—dinner is served. (OK, maybe it's not Food Channel® worthy.)

Cooking and cleaning up can be a lot of work, but, in one way, it reminds me of childbirth: when the meal is produced, and you're sitting around the table enjoying it with your family, you forget about the pain in the preparation for a while. There really is something about food that fills up our hearts as well as our bellies. As a matter of fact, I discovered a fascinating scripture just a few weeks ago: "And I will bring a morsel of bread, that you may refresh your *hearts*" (Genesis 18:5 NKJV; emphasis added.) I had no idea that the concept of "comfort food" was actually biblical.

Have you ever noticed how often Jesus taught His disciples while gathered around the dinner table and how many of these times ended up in the Bible? Here are just a few examples:

> Now it happened, as Jesus sat at the table in the house . . . (Matthew 9:10 NKJV)

> Later He [Jesus] appeared to the eleven as they sat at the table . . . (Mark 16:14 NKJV)

> And those who sat at the table with Him . . . (Luke 7:49 NKJV)

> As He sat at the table with them . . . He took bread . . . (Luke 24:30 NKJV)

> That you may eat and drink at My table in My kingdom . . . (Luke 22:30 NKJV)

The early church continued the tradition of gathering together for worship and fellowship around the dinner table. "And day by day, attending the temple together and breaking bread in their homes, they received their food with glad and generous hearts" (Acts 2:46).

There really is something transcendent about gathering around the table. Jesus thought it was a perfect place to teach His disciples. I think it is a pretty good place to disciple our little ones too. What do you think?

I'm not much of a cook, I don't always prepare healthy meals, and I stink at presentation, but that doesn't stop me from gathering my family around the table and inviting people over to join us. Actually, my absence of a "cooking anointing" is a joke among my family and friends, but they keep coming back. Maybe it is because what our house may lack in cuisine it makes up for in laughter.

I hope, for your friends' and family's sake, that you are a better cook and hostess than I am. But if you aren't, don't let that stop you from heating up something in the microwave, gathering your family around, inviting some friends, and laughing. Laugh about the food if you must, but laugh . . . and make friends . . . and make memories.

Hopefully, this chapter's Rest Stop will provide just the helpful hint you need to get you started. Let's turn the page and find a way to make this cooking thing a bit easier, so we can gather around the table and fill our hearts as well as our bellies.

Cooking—Rest Stop
You're Really Cookin' Now

 Time-Saving Cooking Tips

Cooking has always been a challenge for me, so easy and fast are usually my first priorities for any meal. (I know nutritious should be up there, but I'm just being honest.) Here are some of my best time-saving cooking ideas:

❖ Purchase lean ground beef from a warehouse store in large quantities. Cook it up all at once and freeze so you have it readily available when a recipe calls for ground beef.

❖ Buy chicken, pork, and certain cuts of beef in large quantities at a warehouse store and divide into freezer bags according to family size. Add marinade and label. This allows you to pull out a bag and stick it in the fridge the night before for thawing and have a ready meal by adding rice or potatoes and veggies. Many can be thrown onto a grill for almost instant meals.

❖ If a recipe calls for grated cheese, chopped vegetables, etc., prepare the whole block of cheese and more veggies than you need and refrigerate the rest for a later meal. I love this tip for chopped onions. If I'm going to cry and get my makeup all messy, I don't want to have to do this more than I absolutely have to. Chop up a few onions and store them in the freezer. They taste just as good in the dish, and you don't have to fix your makeup before dinner.

❖ Put together a handful of "pantry meals"—easy ones with ingredients that can either be kept on the shelf or are made from items you always have on hand. These include:

- Meatless spaghetti or other pasta dish

- Chicken casseroles made with canned chicken

- Grilled cheese sandwiches with tomato soup

- Hearty soups with muffins

- Egg dishes

- Macaroni and cheese with turkey-smoked sausage (keep a supply of this precooked meat in the freezer)

- Beans and cornbread

 ## Utilizing the Freezer

❖ Cook two family meal portions *every time* you cook, freezing half. When you're cooking spaghetti sauce, make two huge pots. Eat one and freeze five others. This "cooking in bulk" approach works well for a variety of things, especially beef, chicken, and pasta dishes.

❖ Try the once-a-month cooking plan. Enlist a friend to cook with you the first time and split the meals. To make it even easier on yourself, purchase one of the following books with step-by-step instructions and recipes created especially for freezer cooking:

- *Dinner's in the Freezer* by Jill Bond

- *Frozen Assets: How to Cook for a Day and Eat for a Month* by Deborah Taylor Hough

 ## Meal Planning

Meal planning is key to saving time. Everyone hates starting dinner only to discover you are missing a key ingredient. There are a variety of ways to organize your meal plans. Here are some ideas:

❖ Create an index card file (4x5 cards work best for this, I think) with meals on the front and ingredients on the back. When you're ready to make your grocery list, pull the meal cards you want for the week or month, and use the ingredients list on the backs to make your shopping list.

❖ If you want to use a software program on your computer, you can create all kinds of menu plans, including ingredients for each meal. Check out these available software programs:

Now You're Cooking - www.ffts.com

The Living Cookbook - www.livingcookbook.com

Big Oven - www.bigoven.com

❖ If you like this idea but wish someone else would do all the work, then you must visit www.e-mealz.com.

❖ Other moms have taken the approach of having meals for a whole week on a particular shopping list. They have four to six of these different lists and then just rotate them, grabbing whichever one they want for that week as they head out to the store. These could even be done by category, such as "most economical," "with one special dinner," or "one night eating out."

❖ Home delivery of groceries is also available for minimal or no cost in some areas. This would be a great way to find a little spare time for another activity. Check with local grocers to see what is available in your area.

❖ Before selecting meals for the week, review your calendar. Plan Crockpot meals for busy days, special meals when your afternoon is free, and so on. Make sure you are planning meals that match your schedule.

 ## Cookbooks

I love cookbooks, especially ones that fit with my busy lifestyle and lack of cooking ability. Here's a sample of some of my favorite cookbooks on my kitchen shelf:

❖ *Fix It and Forget about It: Feasting with Your Slow-Cooker* by Dawn Ranck—I love my Crockpot and I was so glad when this cookbook was published so I could advance past stews and pot roast.

❖ *365 Ways to Cook Chicken* by Cheryl Sedeker—I can't tell you how many times I've reached for this book when all I had was a bag of frozen chicken breasts (from Sam's Club) in my freezer. This cookbook is a life-saver.

❖ Sue Gregg cookbooks—Whenever I start feeling convicted about not serving my family healthier meals, I pull out these cookbooks. I highly recommend them if you, like me, want to cook healthier meals but are overwhelmed at the thought of it. These books are hard to find but worth the effort. I recommend simply ordering them from her Web site at www.suegregg.com.

❖ *The Doubleday Cookbook*—This is one of those huge 4,000 + recipe, with hundreds of charts and definition of terms, cookbooks that every kitchen should have. When I simply want to know how to make plain ol' mashed potatoes or how to cook a roast or the ingredients for cookie cutter cookie mix, this is the book I've turned to for decades.

❖ Church cookbooks are great and usually include not only tried-and-true recipes, but quick and easy recipes as well. They are great garage sale finds and a super investment, particularly since most churches produce cookbooks as fund-raising projects.

As you can see, you can make delicious meals and wonderful memories without a lot of skill, time, or money. That's a good thing because I am often lacking in all three of those arenas. I mentioned earlier my lack of expertise in the finance department. In most other areas, Steve and I balance each other out. That is not the case when it comes to money: we are both out of balance—and so are our checkbooks.

God has been so merciful to us in our weakness. We don't deserve it and yet He continues to pull us out of every hole we get ourselves into and provide abundantly for our family. During those times we've hit rock bottom, He was the Rock we landed on and we learned some important lessons while face down on the ground.

We are still learning. Allow me to share some of the lessons God is teaching us.

18

Finances

Have I Got a Retirement Plan for You

I love tithing! That may sound like an odd statement, but it sums up how I feel about money. Giving God 10 percent off the top of everything our family earns is my favorite part. It is not only a privilege to bring the "firstfruits" to the Lord, but, selfishly, I know I can never outgive God.

Luke 6:38 says, "If you give, you will receive. Your gift will return to you in full measure, pressed down, shaken together to make room for more, and running over. Whatever measure you use in giving—large or small—it will be used to measure what is given back to you" (NLT).

The Lord has taught me a lot of lessons in the area of finances, mostly through life experiences, logical consequences, and what-not-to-do lessons learned in the school of hard knocks. I may have failed a few tests, but I definitely retained what I learned.

I've shared many of these stories in colorful detail in some of my other books, so I won't repeat myself here. But I would like to give the Cliffs Notes version to share some background on why I love giving so much.

I mentioned earlier in this book that I lost all of the money I made on *The Facts of Life*. The sad truth about that is, I did all of the right things. I had a business manager, so he invested my money in all the tried-and-true places. I had money in real estate, stocks, homestead, a retirement account, and other financial areas that I don't know enough about to articulate. The bottom line was—I was diversified!

At the height of the show's popularity, I felt the Lord impress upon me to liquidate all of my assets, live on a fraction of what I was making, and give the rest of the money away, specifically to children in Third World countries. Tithing to my local church was a given; I knew God was asking me to go above and beyond and give an overflow offering to His children. I had every intention of obeying God, but eventually "common sense" won out, and I was convinced that giving away my money would be foolish and that I should save my money for the unforeseen future.

To make a long story short, within a few short years, all of that money had disappeared. There was a banking crisis, a real estate collapse, tax law changes, and a bunch of other circumstances that all lined up like the perfect storm to wipe away all of my money.

I understood with grave clarity what Jesus meant when He said, "Store your treasures in heaven, where they will never become moth-eaten or rusty and where they will be safe from thieves" (Matthew 6:20 NLT). Or where asbestos will invade the high-rise you've invested in, or where there will be an oil crisis in Texas where all of your land holdings are, or when you have to give your house back to the bank because the California market is ridiculous!

I used to think that "storing your treasure in heaven" meant giving your money to the church. Then I meditated on that passage and came up with a different interpretation.

Let me ask you a question: where is the only place you can invest your money here on earth that will also be in heaven? Answer: people! God isn't asking us to give our money to the church as an institution or a building but as a community of believers, our brothers and sisters, His children. When we invest our money in people, we are sending our money on ahead to heaven, where it is safe (and pays in dividends).

I realized the Lord hadn't told me to give away all my money because He wanted it. He was being my Wonderful (financial) Counselor and telling me to invest it in the only place it would be safe—heaven. That kind of thinking may sound crazy to the world, but it was God's wise counsel to me.

First Corinthians 1:20 says, "Where is the wise man? Where is the scholar? Where is the philosopher of this age? [Where is the business manager?] Has not God made foolish the wisdom of the world?" (NIV). I learned many expensive but valuable lessons by failing this particular test. Trusting God even when He doesn't make sense was only one of them.

I guess I learned a thing or two, because the next story I want to share is about a time when I actually passed the test and the "smiley face" I received from my Teacher.

One day, I discovered that the Mouseketeer ears I had worn when I was on *The New Mickey Mouse Club* as a child were being auctioned off by Vault Disney on eBay. I was very excited at the prospect of owning "my ears" and passing them down to my children and grandchildren.

During the final minutes of the auction, as I sat poised to send in my bid, I felt the Lord whisper to my heart, "Don't store up for yourself treasures on earth . . . " I thought, *Lord, You couldn't mean my ears!* But I knew it was His voice I was hearing, ever so faintly. I had just finished reading a book called *Money, Possessions, and Eternity* by Randy Alcorn, and I had been asking the Lord for wisdom regarding our finances.[16] But I didn't mean in this case! This was certainly an exception, wasn't it?

Thankfully, I had learned enough to obey God whether He appeared to make sense or not, so I didn't hit the Send key on my bid. Instead, I took the amount of money I was willing to bid on the ears and stored up my money in heaven by sending a check to Compassion International, a child relief organization.

I also sent an e-mail to the gentleman who won the auction and now owned my pink ears, congratulating him and telling him that if he ever decided to sell the ears, I would appreciate it if he contacted me first. (Just in case God changed His mind about my buying them, you know.)

Two weeks later, I received an e-mail from this man. He shared an amazing story with me. Apparently, just as he was putting my mouse ears into storage, the thought popped into his head: *Maybe these ears belong with Lisa and her family.* Not being a particularly religious man, he said to himself, "God, if that is You talking, then You are going to have to do better than that, because I paid seven hundred bucks for these ears."

Immediately, as if on cue, over the speakers in his warehouse, a song "Blaired" out over the speakers. Can you guess which song from the CD of TV theme songs just happened to be next in the rotation? "You take the good, you take the bad, you take them both, and there you have the facts of life, the facts of life." He said that it was in that moment he knew that God wanted me to have those special pink ears, and they were not his to keep any longer.

This is the kind of God we serve! Not one who is always asking for money for Himself, but One who is asking us to give money away so our hands will be open to receive even more from His hand. Now, so far, I've been sharing examples of giving above and beyond because God likes to give back "exceedingly abundantly above all that we ask or think" (Ephesians 3:20 NKJV).

I started out this chapter talking about tithing, which is a bit different. Offerings are simply that: things that we offer to the Lord, for many reasons. We are made in God's image, and we, too, love to give. We've learned that you can't outgive God. We know it simply makes good financial sense to invest in a failsafe plan that keeps on giving for eternity. And on and on.

Tithing, on the other hand, is not *giving* God anything. It is *bringing* to Him what is already His. Everything we have is a gift from God. We have a job and the health to perform it well because of His blessing. It is our duty and privilege to return to God the first 10 percent off the top by giving it to your church home. For one thing, this keeps our heart in the right place and reminds us where our material blessings come from.

Tithing is simply smart business on many levels. Malachi 3:8–9 shows us a conversation between God and His people, Israel, about the importance of tithing: "'Will a man rob God? Yet you rob me. But you ask, "How do we rob you?" In tithes and offerings. You are under a curse—the whole nation of you—because you are robbing me'" (NIV). I love how our pastor, Ed Young Jr. puts it. He says that he and his wife have decided that they would rather have 90 percent blessed money than 100 percent cursed money. Makes sense to me!

There are some who argue that we are no longer living under the Old Testament law, so we are not required to tithe anymore. I'm sure that is a valid argument, and I have no desire to receive a bunch of e-mails from people who want to debate the issue. You win.

On the other hand, if you really want to win, then why would you *not* want to tithe? God continues His conversation with Israel in Malachi 3:10: "'Bring the whole tithe into the storehouse, that there may be food in my house. Test me in this,' says the LORD Almighty, 'and see if I will not throw open the floodgates of heaven and pour out so much blessing that you will not have room enough for it.'" (NIV).

Obviously, I don't want your money. I don't solicit charitable donations, and that is not what I'm after. I'm just so excited about tithing and the blessings I've received that giving 10 percent of your income back to God is the best financial advice I can think to give you in a chapter about money!

I focused on tithing and giving in this chapter because I believe it is the cornerstone for financial freedom. Obviously, there are many more steps and wise building blocks that need to be established if we are to become faithful stewards of the money God has given us.

As we learn more and develop good habits of tithing, saving, investing, budgeting, and wise spending, then we will live less-stressful lives. My desire is that some of the helpful hints in the next Rest Stop will bring peace to your home, family, marriage, and heart. By establishing a few good financial principles, you will be taking care of the "me" in mommy by protecting yourself against the anxiety and turmoil that so often accompany a home where the finances are not in order.

Finances—Rest Stop
When the Budget Won't Budge

 Money-Saving Tips

Here are some of my favorite "everyday" ways to save money:

- ❖ Ask yourself—do I want it or do I need it? This tip alone will double your savings.

- ❖ For further savings ask yourself the following questions:

  - Do I already have something similar I can use instead?

  - How long will I have to work to pay for this?

  - What else could I buy that I really need with this money?

- ❖ Always order water when dining out—this will save lots of money, especially when the whole family goes out.

- ❖ Go to matinee showings of movies and theaters.

- ❖ Eat out of your pantry and freezer for one week.

- ❖ Do a Google® search for "Make Your Own Mixes" and save tons of money by not buying prepackaged mixes for dinner.

❖ Label a jar "vacation" or another activity the whole family will enjoy (like going to the local theme park), and collect all your family's spare change. It's amazing how quickly the jar will fill with coins!

❖ Check out Wal-Mart's policy of matching competitors' prices—this saves time and money!

❖ Before purchasing, rehearse the five Rs—Repair, Restore, Reduce, Reuse, and Recycle. These "R" always helpful when it comes to saving money.

❖ As a rule, never buy on impulse. Discipline yourself to take at least twenty-four hours before you purchase something. You can always go back and get it the next day. In the meantime you have time to pray about it, ask your husband's opinion, see if there are any online reviews, and research for a better price.

❖ Be aware of your emotions when you are shopping. Are you buying something because you are bored? Dissatisfied? You deserve it? If you recognize emotional spending, go home and spend some time feeding your spirit, either in prayer, worship, or reading your Bible. Ask the Lord to fill that need.

❖ Pay attention as your sales clerk rings up your items. We all make mistakes, and it could be a costly one. (You should avoid being on the cell phone in a checkout line, anyway; it is rude.)

❖ Keep a handy list of upcoming birthdays and holidays and shop for gifts all year long.

❖ Don't be ashamed, afraid, or embarrassed to return items that don't fit, don't work, or you simply don't like. (Return as soon as possible, so the store has a chance to resell and you don't miss the return policy window.)

❖ Shop discounted bread stores. Just because they are marked down doesn't mean they are stale or will start growing green stuff within a day. Most of the bakery items are still very fresh.

❖ Create a price book to record frequently purchased items and where to find them least expensively. Visit www.organizedhome.com for a free printable price book sample and how-to instructions.

 ## Coupon Clipping

❖ Use coupons! Not just for food, but for restaurants and services (such as cleaners, nail salons, pet care, and so on). Many stores will also match competitors' coupons and honor expired coupons.

❖ Check out www.grocerygame.com. This Web site saves you time and money by doing most of the coupon-clipping work for you.

❖ There are a variety of other great coupon sites, and many national stores, restaurants, and services post coupons on their Web sites. Before you leave home or even shop on the Internet, type in one of the following Web site addresses and see if there is a money-saving coupon to print out first:

www.coolsavings.com

www.hotcoupons.com

❖ Almost every store offers coupons or promotional prices at one time or another. Before making a purchase or going to a store, visit their Web site and see if they offer coupons to download and print out.

❖ Pay attention to double- and triple-coupon days at the grocery store, and try to shop on those days (with the coupons you've been clipping!).

❖ Entertainment Books have coupons for many restaurants and activities in your local area, and they are great resources for date nights or dinner out with friends. If you need to, find a friend and split the book (www.entertainment.com). You can also download coupons from their Web site.

Technology Tips

❖ I highly recommend investing in personal finance software like Quicken or Microsoft Money! These programs can take much of the headache out of bookkeeping.

❖ Look into online banking. You can set up your monthly bills to be paid automatically which saves you tons of time.

❖ There are also terrific software programs to help you file your own taxes, ultimately saving you time and money. Consider Turbo Tax® by Quicken® or TaxCut ® by H&R Block®.

Alternative Shopping

❖ A great Web site to find almost anything is eBay®! Check there first. You may also want to look for items on Overstock.com® or in the classifieds of your local newspaper.

❖ The Dollar Store can be a great place to shop and save money. When my children were small, every Christmas, Father's Day, and on Steve's birthday, I would give the kids each a dollar and let them buy anything in the store. They felt so big, and their selections were precious. Those gifts are still some of Steve's favorites.

❖ Consignment shops are great for shopping—but also consider selling items there! Limit the amount you spend in the store to what you can earn from selling items there.

❖ You can take "yard sale-ing" to the next level by gathering a handful of friends and pooling your time and energy. The best deals always go first, so target the best yard sales in your area from the newspaper ads, have each person make up her wish list, stay in touch via cell phones, and then have everyone head out bright and early to different locations.

❖ Consider a Christmas job if your schedule will allow it. Many retailers need extra help just on weekends or evenings. Apply to stores where you would like to purchase gifts and you get a double bonus—you have extra holiday income and you can use your employee discount on the presents.

❖ My teenagers tell me that thrift store shopping is all the rage. Hey, take advantage of this phenomenon and go on a shopping spree.

 Money Talk

❖ Steve and I make all major financial decisions together. Marriage is a partnership, and, in this area particularly, it is very important for both spouses to be involved and represented in the decision-making process.

❖ There's no need to make major purchases unless items are on sale. By taking time to research, plan, and negotiate for the best deal, you can save a ton of money and avoid buying on impulse.

❖ Consider doing a month's worth of a "spending journal." This is similar to keeping a journal of everything you eat—and probably just as enlightening!

❖ There is a concern that at some season of our lives, as women we will need to know how to take care of money matters on our own. I encourage you to think about these aspects and, if you haven't already, learn more about retirement planning, IRAs, estate planning, college tuition planning, and income taxes. Community centers and colleges offer courses, many times free of charge.

❖ Build a savings plan into your budget. Plan to have at least three to six months' income as your goal. And if you do experience a financial crisis (layoff, unexpected medical bills, etc.), you won't have to go into debt to survive, which will only cause more anxiety at an already stressful time.

❖ If this is a weaker area of your life, you may need more help than the handful of tips in the Rest Stop. Consider an in-depth Bible study, DVD program, or church-offered class. Ask your pastor for recommendations, or visit some of these godly financial ministries:

www.crown.org

www.daveramsey.com

www.ronblue.com

Or, reading one of the following excellent books on ways to save money, avoid debt, and become a faithful steward of your finances:

- *The Total Money Makeover* by Dave Ramsey

- *Debt-Free Living* by Larry Burkett

- *A Woman's Guide to Financial Peace of Mind* by Ron & Judy Blue

- *The Cheapskate Gourmet* by Mary Hunt

- *Shop, Save, and Share* by Ellie Kay

Don't Neglect Your Financial Spiritual Cornerstones

❖ *Tithe.* You and your spouse, if you are married, need to be accountable to each other to make sure you are following your tithing plan and commitments.

❖ *Offerings.* Children also need to learn about offerings, which are gifts you give back to God over and above your 10 percent tithe. Special times of need or holidays are especially good times to teach them the importance of giving to others and the Lord through praise offerings.

❖ *Missions.* Giving money to support missionaries is one of the easiest ways you can become involved in world evangelism.

I understand that money is an issue for most families. In many homes, the only answer has been for the mom to remain in the workplace. I've found myself on both sides of the garage door. I've loved being a stay-at-home mom, and I've trusted the Lord when I needed to work outside the home. (Yes, I know, all moms are working moms. You know what I mean.)

My heart is especially tender toward single moms. If you are a single mother, I'm so happy to see you reading a book like this. You, of all moms, need to be careful to take care of yourself.

Whether you are married or not, work full-time, part-time, inside the home or out, I hope you find some respite from the stories and tips in the next chapter.

19

Working Moms

The Proverbs 31 Working Woman

I always planned to go back to work after I had my children. I assumed I would simply be able to do it all. I could take my children to the set with me, with a nursery in my trailer and a nanny on board. There was only one problem: I couldn't get hired.

For some reason, after being on a successful television show for nine years, I thought it would be easier to get an acting job, not harder! I went on audition after audition, and nobody would give me a part. I remember after one particularly awful reading for a role, sitting outside the studio in my minivan, I prayed, "Lord, if You didn't want me to have that show, then I'm fine with that. But wasn't there some other way You could've gotten Your point across besides humiliation?"

He gently answered me, *Sweetie, if you haven't noticed, I've removed My hand of blessing from you in show business, and I've moved it to your home and family. If you want to find the success you are looking for, then you need to come over to where I'm working.*

I didn't want to argue with God, but I did want to make sure He had thought this all the way through. So I reminded Him, "But Lord, if I'm not on television, then I won't have the platform to tell the world about You." God very graciously made His point crystal-clear: *Lisa, darling, I can use anybody to tell the world about Me, but I can only use you to be a wife to Steve and a mother to Tucker, Haven, and Clancy.*

That was all I needed to hear. Not only should I not feel guilty about "just being a mom," but I would be disobeying the Lord by not fulfilling the call He had on me for this season of my life. From that moment on, I jumped into my role as full-time wife and mother with both feet and loved every minute of it!

I do believe that God's original design is for women to stay home and serve their husbands and nurture and train their children. I think that is why, as wonderful a life as I had before, it pales in comparison to the contentment and privilege of being a wife and stay-at-home mom.

Even so, I've walked with the Lord long enough not to put Him in the proverbial box. Just as surely as it was His will for me to leave Hollywood, it has been His will in the last few years of my life to go back to work. Interestingly, it was an easier sacrifice to obey Him and leave fame and fortune behind than it has been to give up some of my precious time at home with my family.

For so many reasons, my heart breaks for single moms. They don't even have a choice. They must work or their children won't eat. For that matter, there are many married moms who would love to stay home with their children but simply cannot afford that luxury.

One thing about the Lord, though—He will never ask you to sacrifice something that He doesn't have a plan to give a return. Matthew 19:29 says, "Everyone who has given up houses or brothers or sisters or father or mother or children or property, for my sake, will receive a hundred times as much in return and will have eternal life" (NLT).

This is exactly what happened to me. After a considerable time of grieving the loss of the simple life we had known for ten years, my family chose to trust the Lord with this new direction of my working outside the home as an author/speaker.

One day, my publisher asked me, "We know you gave up show business to stay at home with your family, but you are going to be willing to travel and promote your book, aren't you?" I jokingly answered, "Sure, if I can bring my family with me."

I wasn't so naive to think a church or bookstore would be able to afford five airplane tickets just so my whole family could come. But this offhanded remark got the wheels turning in my head. *What if I could bring my family with me?* That is when what we call "The Family Dream" began.

About a year later, after a series of miracles, Steve, Tucker, Haven, Clancy, and I loaded up in a beautiful RV loaned to us by Tiffin Motorhomes and traveled around the country for a year. We logged more than seventy thousand miles across forty-four states, speaking at various churches on the weekend and appearing at bookstores during the week. We had the time of our lives discovering America and, more importantly, discovering each other.

That is so much like the Lord! What I thought was going to take me away from my family—writing books and speaking—actually afforded me more time with my children and extra time with my husband!

Having experienced both sides of the coin, you won't find me either judging the working mother or looking down my nose at the stay-at-home mom. There's isn't any need to look further than the famous Proverbs 31 woman to see that the Lord affirms stay-at-home moms *and* moms who work outside the home.

Mrs. Proverbs 31 was definitely a working mother. She bought real estate, took the equity and established a vineyard, ran her own home business making belts and selling them, had a maid, shopped for bargains, sewed her own clothes, was in the ministry, bought the freshest produce to feed her family, worked out, and organized her household. (Read it in your Bible; it is all there.)

It is my personal opinion that she didn't do all of these things at the same time. She couldn't have! We all have tried it and know that it just isn't physically, emotionally, or spiritually possible. I believe Mrs. P. did all these things over the course of her married life. At different seasons of her life she focused on different priorities.

I think that is the key. Paying attention to the seasons and listening to the Creator of the seasons for direction. There is a time for everything. It is our responsibility to ask the real "Father Time" for the wisdom to know which season of life we are currently in and keep us sensitive when the temperature begins to change. I understand there are many women who would love to stay home with their kids, but because of circumstances beyond their control they must work outside the home.

More than any other group, moms who work outside the home must force themselves to take time for the "me" in mommy. Notice I said "take" time. There just aren't enough hours in the day to wait until you have a few minutes to spare for yourself. It won't happen.

Trust me on this, your children would rather have a bit less time with a refreshed and rejuvenated mom then every available minute with a mother who is frazzled, irritable, and completely sucked dry.

It can also be extremely stressful living on one income, no matter how much you enjoy being at home with your children. That is why in the following Rest Stop I've included tips to help working mothers balance their career with their families, as well as ideas for stay-at-home moms to contribute to the family income with a home-based businesses.

My prayer is that one of these ideas will buy you a few extra minutes of refreshment so you can enjoy your work and your family—and your family can enjoy a well-balanced mom.

Working Moms—Rest Stop Juggling Tips

Is Staying at Home an Option?

Last night I was having a difficult time getting back to sleep after a mid-dle-of-the-night, this-bladder-has-suffered-through-one-too-many-children-potty break. For some strange reason, I started thinking about dying. After much morbid contemplation I realized, as much as I would miss seeing my children become adults, meeting their spouses, and enjoying my grandchildren, I could die tonight and be at peace. I feel like I've done my job.

Ironically, as much as I believe I'm making a difference with the books I'm writing and the places I'm speaking and although I know that my years on *The Facts of Life* were all part of God's plan for my life, these last sixteen years raising my children feel like the most important years I've spent.

Hopefully, I have the rest of my life to make other eternal investments in the kingdom, but I doubt anything will be of more value than the time I took to invest in teaching my children about the ways of the Lord.

It is not my heart to make anyone feel guilty for working outside of the home, especially single moms. Please believe me on this. But if it is even remotely possible, taking a miracle-working God into consideration, could you see if there is any way to make it work with you staying at home when your children are small? Begin by taking an objective look at the income you are realistically adding to your family. If you need help evaluating your particular situation, take the salary you are bringing in and deduct the following work-related expenses:

❖ Federal taxes

❖ State taxes

❖ Local taxes

❖ Social Security

❖ Medicare tax

❖ Child care

❖ Commuting (toll, parking, second car)

❖ Gasoline and mileage

❖ Car insurance (extra car, nicer car)

❖ Clothing expenses (dry-cleaning, new)

❖ Gifts for co-workers

❖ Convenience food for meals

❖ Eating out

❖ Housekeeping help

❖ Extra cost related to lack of time to research cheaper prices

❖ Extra cost related to hiring help instead of making repairs yourself

Most of the time, moms work because of the family's financial demands. But by redefining *needs* and actually calculating what your working outside the home costs the family, you can sometimes see more benefits to staying home.

 ## Would a Part-Time Job Be Enough?

My next question for you is, how much work do you need to do to generate the income needed? Part-time and seasonal employment may suffice. Here are some suggestions:

❖ Working at a Parents' Day Out or Mothers' Day Out program (or other child care programs that offer child care for your child, perhaps with your being able to be with your child while earning extra income).

❖ Live-in care facilities for children and elderly often need people who sleep at the facility one or two nights a week in case emergencies arise while primary staff are away. Many nights go uninterrupted, so you can juggle your sleep needs. This is a great part-time income for Mom because Dad is at home with the kids.

❖ Stagger work schedules so either Mom or Dad is home with the kids. This requires more work, but not putting the kids in someone else's care is worth the effort. But be careful to have a support system in place so you can nurture your marriage rather than simply saying hello as you pass each other on your way to work.

❖ Consider teaching or being a teacher's aide if you need to work outside the home. It allows your schedule to flow with the kids' schedule, giving you summers and holiday breaks to enjoy being a full-time mom.

 # Home-Based Businesses

Is it possible to work from your home? Have you considered any of these areas?

❖ Child care services in your home

❖ Buy items at garage sales and resell them for profit on eBay or sign up to be an eBay Trading Assistant and sell other people's "junk" for a commission.

❖ Find Internet jobs, learn Web design or graphic design, or find another career that can be done from your computer.

❖ Consider catering, birthday and wedding cakes, event planning, or other home-based businesses that make use of one of your particular skills.

❖ Bookkeeping and accounting jobs are great part-time income earners.

❖ Home-based companies such as:

> Mary Kay®
>
> Pampered Chef®
>
> Arbonne®
>
> Amway®
>
> Premiere Jewelry®
>
> Tupperware®
>
> Creative Memories®

Stampin' Up®

Usborne Books®

Southern Living at Home®

Tips for Working at Home

If you establish a work-from-home business, as I have in the last several years, consider these tips:

❖ Keep a schedule with definite work hours and time off to be with the kids. Without this routine, you may end up off balance and very frustrated. For young children, this may mean hiring child care. Consider Parents' Day Out programs, which are usually only twelve to eighteen hours a week, or hire a homeschooled teenager for the task.

❖ Let the business answering machine screen calls, and have set times when you answer the phone.

❖ Leave a recorded "out to lunch" message and go have lunch with your children.

❖ Forward your office phone calls to your cell phone if you must run an errand or pick up a child.

❖ Have a secluded space to work, away from the hub of the home, if possible. Even a walk-in closet can serve as an office. Do not use the kitchen table as an office. It leads to frustration for the entire family!

❖ Have a work e-mail as well as a personal one. Only check your work e-mail during work hours to keep from getting distracted (and vice versa).

❖ Communicate often and openly about your schedule. Give your family an opportunity to express their frustrations or feelings, and try to work out compromises, explaining the need for household income generated from your work time. Thank them for their understanding and cooperation regularly.

❖ Kids can do a lot more than we often give them credit for. Let them take on chores and responsibilities.

❖ Keep a notepad or notebook handy so you can jot down work-related notes when you're "off work." This will keep you from going back into your work area and getting involved during times you've set aside for your family.

❖ Having only one calendar works best for me, though I know some people prefer to keep two calendars: one for home and one for work.

 ## The Business Line

If you work out of your home, you probably spend the majority of your work day on the phone. Since kids think Mommy picking up the phone is their cue to act up, you may want to implement a few of these ideas:

❖ When you know you are about to make an important phone call, ask your child if there is anything he or she need before you get on the phone. Then explain that, if something comes up, unless it is an emergency (you may need to define *emergency*) the child will need to wait until you hang up.

❖ Teach your children certain hand signals to let them know you are on a business call and they absolutely must be quiet.

❖ Be sure and take the time after you hang up to compliment your child for being so patient and follow through on listening to his/her need. Or you may need to take the time to correct him or her for not being quiet when you gave them the understood signal.

❖ If your kids are crying or the siblings are fighting when the phone rings, let it go to voice mail. It is better to return the call in a few minutes than have the unprofessional background noise.

 ## When You Have to Work Outside the Home

When there are no other alternatives, here are some survival tips for moms who work outside the home:

❖ Two words—*Routine* and *Meal Planning*. Okay, that's two ideas and three words.

❖ Get up before everyone to have some quiet time with the Lord. Keep a notepad beside you to jot down "to do" items that come to your mind so you are not tempted to stop praying and run to the computer.

❖ Spend commute time wisely. Put on a worship CD or Bible tape or sermon message.

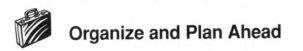 ## Organize and Plan Ahead

❖ Be proactive about being organized. Life will run you if you don't run all of your responsibilities. Keeping a master calendar and tracking progress of priorities will be critical to your success.

❖ Grocery shopping can be divided into "major shopping" and "minor stops." A couple of times a week, keep bread and milk supplied, plus fresh vegetables and items you run out of between "major shopping" trips. Make your goal to do major shopping only once a month. Use a master grocery list for this trip, purchasing in bulk as much as possible.

❖ Pack a lunch and spend breaks and lunch times working on household items. These might include scheduling appointments, hiring sitters, and printing research materials for children's home-work assignments.

❖ Ask your employer if you can adjust your work schedule, perhaps reducing your total hours to thirty-five hours. Sometimes, working longer days but only four days a week works well. Or perhaps trad-ing an afternoon midweek with a Saturday morning might be a better solution for the family's needs. All of these minor adjust-ments can reap large benefits toward your goals as a "mom."

❖ Plan your morning and do as much as you can the night before. Lay out lunches, outfits, backpacks, briefcase, etc. This helps keep the stress level down in the morning so everyone can start his/her day more relaxed.

 ## Share the Load

❖ Divide household chores with your husband, since both of you will need to pitch in to keep the house in order. Make sure the kids do their part. Assign chores and post a chart so everyone can stay on track.

❖ Make a pact with your husband: until after the kids are in bed, you both must resist the need to "veg" when you get home. This not only allows you to get everything accom-plished nightly, but also allows you time to spend with your kids—working on homework, having dinner together, reading them bedtime stories, and so on.

❖ Choose one night a week where you and your husband hire a sitter and spend the evening alone. If you both work outside the home, your time together will be even more difficult to accomplish, and you will have more issues that need both of your input and focus. This evening can be part planning and part fun—but regular, routine time together alone is essential to keeping the house running smoothly and your children's emotional and physical needs met.

❖ If possible, consider alternating schedules with your husband so one of you gets the kids off in the morning and goes into work later while the other one picks them up from school and gets homework and dinner started. This will maximize your time expenditure on those two major daily tasks and give your kids after-school time with Mom or Dad, freeing up evening time for more family interaction.

 Family Time and Other Priorities

❖ Be very selective about your expectations and priorities. Don't expect to keep up the same pace as families who have a stay-at-home mom. Have a master plan with your husband, if married, about how your home can remain centered and focused without your contribution as a stay-at-home mom.

❖ Your weekend priority has to be family time, though you can be creative about how to accomplish quality family time with household chores and kids' activities. But you must constantly prioritize family time above all other activities.

❖ TV watching in the evenings and on weekends has to be kept to a minimum, since it prevents family interaction and accomplishing household chores. Tape favorite shows and watch them later—it also saves time because you can skip the commercials!

❖ Schedule specific times on the weekends, perhaps midafternoon naps, when you can catch a few extra hours of sleep.

❖ Budget days or half days throughout the year when you take time off that is yours alone. Spend those special times on yourself!

❖ Find another working mother and swap out kids for weekend get-aways once or twice a year with your husband. You will need to make time for romance—don't neglect this important aspect of your relationship.

Not only is it imperative to prioritize family in the midst of our busy days, but we must also be intentional about nurturing our friendships with other women. Whether you work outside the home or rarely find yourself leaving the home, all women need good girlfriends. This is not just about having coffee with a friend, going shopping with your mom or meeting a group of gals for lunch.

Friendship is life giving. Yes, as the fabulous praise song goes, "I am a friend of God." And, I know, our husbands are supposed to be our best, best friends. Still, there is nothing that can take the place of a good girlfriend. If you don't have one, you must get one! (I'll pray with you about this.) If you do have one, then you must invest in your relationship. I promise, your family will reap the benefits.

part
5

Finding Time for Each Other

20

Friends

Networking

A few years ago, our family moved from California to Texas. This was a huge transition for each of us. Steve was no longer working full-time for the church where he had attended and been employed for almost thirty years. Our children, who were all in junior high, were leaving behind best friends whom they had known since they were in playpens. And I was saying goodbye to the only girlfriends I had ever had.

I know that may sound dramatic, but it was true. I was never very popular in school growing up, I worked all through my teenage years, and from as far back as I can remember, my mother has always been my best friend. I really didn't think I needed any other friends. Between my husband and my mom, I thought I had it covered in the friendship department.

Then I started my MomTime group, and for the first time in my life I had bona fide girlfriends. I hadn't known what I was missing! I met every Friday with these ladies for more than ten years. We were there for each other through the births of babies and the deaths of loved ones. Some of us were great cooks, and others of us were great eaters. We took turns making each other laugh or offering shoulders on which to cry.

I've dedicated this book to these friends because there have been many times I don't know how I would have gotten through some of the tough times without their support. When my marriage was barely hanging on by a thread, I ran to my friends, and they listened, prayed, held me accountable, and stood by my side. When my little girl had open-heart surgery, they rallied around us. When I bit off more than I could chew and had a book deadline, too many speaking engagements, and three kids to homeschool, they jumped in and helped carry the load.

In between the valleys of life, we laughed on the mountains. We had Christmas parties, murder mystery evenings, progressive dinners, and girlfriend getaways. I learned how to cook from Connie, how to throw a party from Sallie, how to be a friend from Shawn, how to laugh from Andrea, how to be yourself from Valerie, how to create a lovely home from Denise, and deep goodness from Deb. We talked about toddlers and teenagers, husbands and "headaches," PMS and ADD, and everything in between.

Looking back over these times and many more like them, I am so grateful God gave me friends. I'm also thankful I took the time to nurture those friendships on a consistent basis so the relationships were strong and in place when the storms of life inevitably came. I can only imagine how tossed around and alone I would have felt going through some of the tougher times without a safety net of girlfriends.

That is why one of my first orders of business when we moved to Texas was to start another MomTime group in my home. I had lived life *with* girlfriends and *without* them, and I had learned how much fuller life can be with a gaggle of gals around you. The big question was, where was I going to find these new friends? I think it is so much easier to make friends when your children are younger. You meet other moms at playgroups, Little League, and parenting classes. You are all in the same stage of life and have so much in common that it is very easy to strike up a conversation and begin a friendship.

This was going to be tougher the second time around. My children were older, they were homeschooled, we hadn't yet found a church home, and ours was only one of three houses built on our block. I only knew one other person in the area, so I asked her if she would like to come over for lunch . . . and would she mind bringing some of her friends to join us?

A few days later, I happened to be out at the mailbox at the same time our neighbor across the street was getting her mail, so I asked if she would like to join us for lunch sometime. We eventually found a church home, so I invited the student pastor's wife to join us for fun and games the following week. Next, a young mom came knocking on my door asking if my daughter could baby-sit. I said, "Sure, and do you think you could come over to my house and play someday too?"

I love my new MomTime group. Because of it, I have friends in their twenties who are popping out babies, friends in their fifties who are dropping off their babies at college, and friends who are my age who simply feel like "popping and dropping" their kids during these teenage years.

In this day and age, it is very difficult to cultivate friendships. We are all so busy. Relationships take time, and we just don't have the time to chat on the phone, pop in unexpectedly for tea, or talk over the fence while gardening. If we are going to develop friendships, we have to write them on our calendars, schedule them in our day planners, and input them into our PDAs.

I'd like to borrow a word from the business circle—"networking." It takes work but we must build a safety net of friends. You think I'm joking, but I'm not. We must be intentional about planting seeds for potential friendships and taking deliberate steps to grow those relationships. You can't wait until you are going through hard times to realize you don't have any emotional support, or a friend to keep your kids, or someone to bring over a meal, or even something as simple as knowing someone else in your life is going to care enough to call, ask how you're doing, and offer to pray with you over the phone.

Ecclesiastes 4:9–10 says, "Two people can accomplish more than twice as much as one; they get a better return for their labor. If one person falls, the other can reach out and help. But people who are alone when they fall are in real trouble" (NLT).

I beg you to make the effort to develop new friendships and nurture the ones you have. I know you don't have time; none of us does. Make time. Women need friends. Moms *really* need friends. Single moms *desperately* need friends. I beg you, please, do everything you can to sustain your friendships with other women. You need the support, emotionally and practically.

If not this very minute, there will come a time when our ability to get up and move on depends on whether we have friends beside us to lift us up. One of the best ways you can take care of yourself is to develop and enjoy being friends with other women.

In the following Rest Stop, I've listed a whole bunch of ways to nurture and develop friendships in your life. But remember, only you can take the time to make the time.

Friends—Rest Stop
Can You Come Over to My House and Play?

Seek out friends and people who are excited about life. If you have friends going through difficult things, help them seek out encouraging situations. If you have friends who drain you emotionally, learn to manage your time with them or seek upbeat mutual friends when you spend time with the hurting friend. This will keep you from being "pulled down" emotionally.

 Phone a Friend

Here are some ideas for fitting friendships into your busy days:

❖ Call one friend each day or at least one friend each week.

❖ With cell phones' unlimited minutes and low-cost long-distance plans, it's easier than ever to stay in touch with good friends. Start the conversation with, "I only have a few minutes, but I wanted you to know I was thinking about you." This way, you can talk for a while but not feel guilty when you can't linger.

❖ Don't neglect family relationships. Call your siblings, parents— even aunts, cousins—occasionally to check on them.

❖ Use a cordless phone or headset and talk to friends while you are cleaning or preparing meals. The headset will be a great invest-ment in keeping your relationships alive.

❖ Don't be afraid to reach out and tell your friends you need their help. Whether it's when you or the kids are sick, when you are emotionally wrung out, or when you just need someone to talk to—you want them to call on you, so don't be afraid to reach out. Many times friendships get distant or languish because no one reaches out.

 ## E-mail and Snail Mail

❖ With e-mail, you can easily write to several people at once, shar-ing details of your household with friends. You can use the same basic content and add a personal paragraph or two for each recipient.

❖ Another great idea is to pray over the Christmas cards you receive, dividing them into the weeks or months of the year and dropping your friends notes when their turn comes up. You can purchase postcards ready to run through your computer printer and design something that says, "We prayed for you this week." Then, all you need to do is add a couple of handwritten lines. Your friends will appreciate the prayer, and many will write back as well. Kids can help and will really enjoy this activity.

❖ Find an "affinity" group online, like parents of twins, kids with ADHD, bipolar teens, etc. Knowing someone understands what you are going through crosses technological boundaries. On-line friendships are perfect for moms of younger children who are not able to get out of the house often to meet up with friends.

Group Friendships

❖ Start a "Pray and Play" group. The kids play while the moms pray and share.

❖ When you sign up the kids for soccer league, church activity, or a YMCA program, sign yourself up for something that meets at the same time. This will force you to make new friends.

❖ If you are the mother of a preschooler, then I highly recommend you join a MOPS group. I can't say enough about this support and resource organization! Go to www.mops.org to check it out.

❖ Join a Bible study at your local church—or at a church near your house where you'll meet new friends, hopefully in your neighborhood. Most have child care built into their programs, so your kids will be making new friends too.

❖ Host a Bunco night. Bunco is a great party game that requires little thought but results in much laughter.

❖ Start a MomTime Group (see my Web site for details on how to get started).

I mentioned earlier that I will pray with you if you don't have a good girlfriend. I mean that. I have already prayed for you, and I will continue. My tongue was only partially in my cheek when I made the crack about our husbands being our best, best friends. I really do mean that too.

I can honestly say that Steve is my very best, best friend. I couldn't always say that. (Well, I could have said it but I would have been lying, and I am supposed to be writing a Christian book.) It has taken a lot of years of hard work for us to get to this place, but it is better than I even could have imagined.

Your husband may already be your best friend. If that is the case then I hope you find some ideas for making your relationship even stronger. If you are where I was about a decade ago, then I hope you'll believe me when I assure you that all things are possible with God. I've already written about that miracle in my autobiography. Allow me to share some of the more recent lessons the Lord is teaching me in the area of marriage. (By the way, if you don't have a husband, I'll pray about that too, if you want me to.)

21

Marriage

Date Your Mate

*M*ost every Friday morning you'll find me flying somewhere to speak, and I'm usually back on a plane Saturday night heading home. We moved from Los Angeles to Dallas to cut down on travel time by flying out of the center of the country.

Before the move, Steve and I would typically wake up around three o'clock on Friday morning in order to make the hour drive to the airport to catch a six o'clock flight. We would usually cross at least two time zones and arrive in a city with just enough time to change clothes, freshen up my makeup, and head to the church where I was scheduled to speak that evening.

The next morning, our hotel wake-up call would ring way too early for our Pacific Coast time-zoned bodies, and we would hop out of bed (OK, so we didn't exactly hop), shower, and get to the church for a full day of ministry. We were rarely able to find a flight back to Los Angeles that evening, so we usually went out to dinner with the pastor's family and then went back to the hotel to enjoy an adult movie. (Hey, relax—to us, that means anything that isn't Disney!) There were way too many Sunday mornings we had to miss attending church as a family.

We knew if we were going to continue with this ministry without sacrificing our family, we were going to have to make some serious changes. The move to Texas was the first of many necessary adjustments. Turning down most invitations that required more than one night away from the children was another decision we knew we had to make. Because we still homeschool, it has also been important that we travel during the week only occasionally.

One of the seemingly obvious choices would be for Steve to stay home with the children while I travel on the weekends. That way, the kids still have one parent at home to keep stability and continuity. We seriously considered this but decided against it. Yes, it would definitely be better for the children, but would it be the best thing for our marriage?

I would be flying off each weekend, meeting interesting people, eating out, staying in hotels, and enjoying new experiences. He would remain at home to wash the dishes, help with schoolwork, run the taxi service, and cook the meals, or more realistically, pick up the fast food. We were concerned that it would be too easy for Steve and me to grow apart, and there were too many obvious places resentment could creep in for either one of us.

We determined that, in the long run, our kids would benefit even more from Steve and me having a strong, healthy marriage than having one parent in the home and one traveling across America. Now we wondered why we labored so long with this decision. Between their grandmother and a handful of wonderful college students from our church, the kids barely even know we're gone anymore.

I hate leaving my children every time I travel for business, but I love the time away with my husband. The Lord has turned what could have been a negative into a positive. We take advantage of the long drives for deep conversation, airport meals for mini dates, and hotel rooms for noisy . . . sleeping. There is also something uniquely uniting about ministering together as a couple.

The weekends are still work, though, so we are also very careful to make sure we set aside one night a week as "date night." Through the years, we have found a number of creative ways to make this happen on a limited budget. When our children were very young, we would put them to bed very early to insure that we had some grown-up time while we could still keep our eyes open.

Once we discovered AWANA (a Scripture-memory program hosted at neighborhood churches), we were able to have a consistent date night every Monday night. We would drop the kids off at church, where they would play games, eat snacks, say their Bible verses, and receive their rewards while Steve and I went out to dinner and reconnected as a husband and wife, not just Mommy and Daddy.

These days we attend a church that only has a midweek service once a month, so Wednesday nights are our new date nights while our children are at youth group. More often than not, Tucker, Haven, and Clancy are playing in the student worship band and have to be at sound check by five o'clock. That means Steve and I have plenty of time to eat dinner, catch a movie, do some shopping, or come back home and enjoy the house all to ourselves.

Staying connected to our spouse takes hard work. I like the way the English Standard Version translates Matthew 19:5–6: " 'Therefore a man shall leave his father and his mother and *hold fast* to his wife, and they shall become one flesh'. . . So they are no longer two but one flesh. What therefore God has joined together, let not man separate" (emphasis added).

We must hold on tightly to our marriages or we will inevitably begin to separate. Picture your husband and yourself on a merry-go-round that feels like it is spinning out of control. (This isn't difficult to imagine, is it? Most of us feel this way quite often.) In order to stay together without falling off, you must do two things: hold on tightly to one another as one and stay close to the center.

Do you see the parallel? If we relax even for a minute, we will find ourselves separating from one another and in danger of becoming another divorce statistic. Our marriages don't stand a chance in this fast-paced world unless we purposely hold fast to one another and make Jesus the Center of our world.

It is true what they say: "The best thing a father can do for his children is to love their mother." I want to make up a new cliché. The best thing a mother can do for her children is to take care of the "me" in mommy and the "pair" in parents.

This can be true even if you have suffered the tragedy of divorce. Just because your children's father doesn't live in the same home doesn't mean you've blown your chances of being a good mom. It gives you that much more opportunity to demonstrate love and grace and forgiveness to your ex-husband. How you relate to him sets an example for your kids.

By taking care of that relationship, you will be giving your children an invaluable gift. You will also be taking care of yourself by letting go of some of the energy it takes to hold on to grudges. You may even find some relief and refreshing practical ways as your ex-husband helps carry the load you typically bear alone. Read through the following Rest Stop and make plans to implement one or more of the ideas to love your children by loving your husband. (There are even a few ideas for ways to love your ex.)

Marriage—Rest Stop
Marriage Glue

Just like every other living organism (I said *organism*; get your mind out of the gutter!) needs care and nutrients to survive, our marriage relationships must have nurture to thrive. So I've divided this Rest Stop into categories that remind us to focus on caring for this vital relationship.

 ## Marriage Vitamins

❖ Invest in a yearly marriage devotional, and plan a time daily when you can spend fifteen minutes doing it together.

❖ Find a book of mutual interest, and take turns reading it to each other every night.

❖ From early on, put your kids on a bedtime schedule. We used 7:00 for preschool kids; 8:00 for elementary; 9:00 for junior high; 10:00 for high school (but must be in room by 9:00). This may sound extreme, but as they got older we made it clear that if they didn't go to sleep right away, that was fine. They just had to stay in their rooms and do quiet activities. This gave Steve and me time to spend with each other, which was a real lifeline for me, especially when the kids were little.

❖ After the kids are in bed, do something physical to help you switch from "mommy mode" to "wife mode," such as taking a hot bath, putting on lipstick, dabbing on perfume, or changing clothes.

❖ Make your bedroom special—keep it clean and add candles or pretty sheets. Make it a sanctuary where the two of you can share your special moments alone.

❖ Show affection! Kiss and hug each other often—it not only keeps you in touch, but it gives the kids a great example.

❖ Don't stay up late doing housework or office work or even a hobby. Go to bed with your husband! Even if you don't fall asleep, you can read or pray together.

❖ Schedule a time during the day for your "chat session." Make sure you still talk!

❖ Go on a "porch-swing date" or a long walk with your husband, and spend time talking and laughing.

❖ Find a hobby you and your husband both enjoy, so some of that time can be together time.

❖ Consider weekend seminars and retreats. Your marriage need not be "in trouble" before you consider these life-enriching experiences.

❖ Do focused Bible studies together. If your marriage is struggling in an area—such as anger, conflict over finances, communication— find a Bible study related to the topic and work through it together.

❖ Plan a pre-Christmas getaway where you can relax before the hectic holidays and shop for the kids.

❖ Read a book on marriage together:

- *Sacred Marriage* by Gary Thomas

- *Love and Respect* by Emerson Eggerichs

- *Hidden Keys of a Loving, Lasting Marriage* by Gary Smalley

- *Quiet Times for Couples* by H. Norman Wright

- And my favorite, *As For Me and My House* by Walter Wangerin

 ## Date Night

Date night, date night, date night! I can't stress enough how much I believe in this habit. I hope all married couples will consider making it an event each week. But it certainly needs to happen twice a month. Here are my favorite ideas:

❖ Hire the sitter to come an hour before you need to leave. This allows you to get ready in peace, and it gives the kids time to adjust to the sitter. It may cost a few dollars more, but it's worth it.

❖ Who says a date has to be away from home? Take the kids to Grandma's house and return home for an intimate evening.

❖ Have lunch with your spouse once a month (no restaurants that give out crayons).

❖ Cheap date-night ideas are plentiful—be creative! The important thing is finding time to talk and communicate your love to each other:

- Go to the dollar movie theater.

- Get an ice cream cone at the mall.

- Look at model homes, collecting ideas and dreaming.

- Test-drive a new vehicle.

- Starbucks coffee and talk time is a great way to reconnect.

 ## Babysitters

The key to date-night discipline, and many of the other suggestions in this book, is a database of several baby-sitters. See the Appendix for tips on how to find trustworthy and reliable baby-sitters.

 ## Sexual Health

Your sexual relationship has to be openly discussed and dealt with. Marriages cannot thrive unless sexual relationship thrives. This does not mean your physical relationship will always be "hot and heavy"! Thriving at forty is very different from thriving at twenty-five. Children present different challenges in this area at different stages of your family life. As your seasons change, expectations and desire may not always be in sync. Here are some ideas:

❖ Openly communicate with each other in a loving and honest way. This is the foundation of sexual closeness.

❖ Grandparents can be a huge blessing to provide a night away for you and your husband. Keep a bag packed and ready for "let us take the kids tonight" opportunities. Pack your nighttime duds, massage oil, candles, perfume, and other things that will help rekindle your love and passion. The truth is, you can get a hotel room for about the same price as a nice dinner out and a movie. Instead of the traditional date, pack a picnic, book a room, hang out in the hot tub, watch a movie in the room, and pretend you are on your honeymoon again.

❖ Do it for your health! Having sex strengthens the immune system by increasing the flow of certain chemicals, which keeps your body healthy. Sex is also exercise, with all of the benefits of lowering cholesterol, increasing circulation, keeping your heart strong, burning calories, and releasing those yummy endorphins.

❖ Seek professional help if either of you becomes unable to express feelings openly or if your physical relationship becomes strained or difficult. This gift of intimacy requires special care to maintain vitality over the course of your married lives.

❖ Read one of following books together, and don't just talk about it:

Intended for Pleasure by Ed Wheat, M.D. and Gaye Wheat

Sheet Music by Dr. Kevin Leman

The Act of Marriage by Tim and Beverly LaHaye

Communication Is Essential

As important as it is to connect physically, it is equally important to connect emotionally. Here are a few bullet-point tips for effective communication. You may want to share this list with your husband. (Tell him Lisa told you to do this. You may also want to show him the "sex list" or one of the books I've suggested, so he knows you're not picking on him.)

❖ Turn off the TV, put down the magazine, turn away from the computer screen, or stop washing the dishes.

❖ Don't let the children interrupt. Show your spouse respect by putting him above the kids.

❖ While listening, respond with sounds and words that assure the other person that you are actively engaged in the conversation.

❖ Try not to think about what you are going to say next. Discipline yourself to listen with your heart to discern your spouse's heart.

❖ Don't offer advice unless asked for it.

❖ Ask questions for clarification or deeper understanding. This is very affirming to know that your spouse isn't just waiting for you to shut up so he or she can say something or move on. By asking a follow-up question, you are communicating that you not only aren't in a hurry, but you want to take all the time you need to understand what he or she is saying.

❖ Before you respond, say, "So, what I hear you saying is . . ." Many times, especially during emotional conversations, communication lines get garbled. By repeating what you think you've heard you can avoid potential miscommunication, and you are more likely to really listen before speaking.

 ## Deeper Issues

If you are experiencing routine symptoms which point to more serious problems under the surface of your marriage, you may need some focused time to determine what is creating the issues. For more serious problems, a series of marriage-counseling sessions may give you the insight you need. Check with your pastor or do an Internet search for Christian counseling centers in your area.

Going to a marriage counselor doesn't necessarily mean your marriage is in crisis. These strategic times—set aside where you can focus on dealing with the issues and their root causes—can greatly strengthen your marriage and put you on a correction course before the underlying causes shipwreck your relationship.

Unfortunately, just like medical tests or hospitalization, none of us relishes the idea of going through the pain or inconvenience to take care of the problems. But don't neglect the most important relationship you have in this earthly life! And if your husband is unwilling to engage in the process, gently try to find someone who can influence him toward health—like a pastor, male mentor, or close friend.

"For when I am weak, then I am strong" (2 Corinthians 12:10). Do you love that verse as much as I do? Whether it is marriage counseling, or crying out to the Lord, or calling a friend for a cup of sugar, there is nothing wrong with asking for help. As a matter of fact, there is everything right about it.

I was just telling my husband this afternoon, "I have absolutely no intention of ever writing a book about parenting teenagers! I am not in any position to give advice." He gently responded, "Haven't all of your books been more about the lessons you have learned from your failures rather than your parenting perfection?" Good point.

If I were to boil down my heart's message to moms, it would probably be this next chapter.

22

Ask for Help

Failure Is a Good Thing

*A*ll I asked for was a little bit of peace and quiet without interruption. I was writing my "MomTime" column for *Today's Christian Woman*, and the deadline to turn it in had already come and gone. I huddled Tucker, Haven, and Clancy together in the family room and explained that I needed them to watch television, read, or play outside. I didn't really care what they did, as long as they would occupy themselves long enough for me to finish this task, and then I would clock back in as "Mom."

I sat down at my computer screen and prayed for wisdom on how to answer these tough parenting questions. I felt so much pressure. Why were these people writing to me for parenting advice, and who was I to think I could answer them? I had never personally dealt with half of these issues, and on the ones I had, the best advice I had to offer was what I had learned from my mistakes. So I kept praying.

I finally launched into my first question, trusting God to give me His wisdom to answer this dear parent. I barely got the first paragraph written when I heard a crisis brewing in the family room. I got up and headed into the other room to referee. Successfully banishing the children into separate corners of the house, I resumed my work.

Halfway into the second paragraph, I heard a scream. I ran upstairs to find two of my children struggling over the same shirt until I thought it would surely rip in half. "It's mine!" "No, it's not!" "I had it first!" "No, you didn't!" I considered declaring it a "jump ball" by throwing the shirt into the air to see who could swat it down first, but instead I chose to do a little swatting myself.

With the shirt in question safely in my possession for the time being, I sat back down to write. Now where was I? Oh yeah, giving parenting advice for a national magazine. How ironic. This time I got all the way through the first question and was answering the second one when a blur ran quickly past the office door, followed by another blur, only this one was shrieking.

I followed the cries out into the backyard, where they were joined by another screeching blur running in the opposite direction. I did what any good mother would do—I yelled at the top of my lungs and told them to stop screaming.

I then proceeded to jump up and down, waving my arms in the air and shouting, "Can't you kids get along for five minutes? YOU ARE OUT OF CONTROOOOOOOL!" I then took off and chased them all the way back into the house and up the stairs as they scurried for their lives into the safety of their rooms.

Later that night, when I put them each to bed, I knew I had to apologize. I started with Clancy and confessed that I was the one who was out of control, that I had put off my writing until the last minute and then unfairly vented my frustration on them.

Now, before I tell you how she responded, I must admit that Clancy came out of the womb perfect. I'm serious. I distinctly remember laying her down in her crib for a nap. She would look up at me, and I could see in her eyes that she was saying, "Well, I'm not really sleepy right now, but you look like you could use a nap, Mommy, so I'll just lie here quietly until you come pick me up again."

You don't believe me, but it's true. Although, I have learned it is best not to attempt to take any of the glory for Clancy, as my easier child. In turn, I won't feel so guilty about my more challenging one.

After my repentance that night, Clancy replied, "Oh no, Mommy, it was our fault. You were simply trying to minister to other moms, and we were being insensitive by fighting." I was feeling better already.

I then walked into Tucker's room. I knew that it was important that I model repentance without offering excuses, blame, or pointing out the other person's wrong to justify my behavior. For my vulnerability I was rewarded with Tucker's response: "What I wouldn't have given to have had a camera in the backyard! I would have taken a picture of you and posted it on your Web site with the caption, 'Parenting Author Loses It!'" Tucker always knows how to make me laugh.

Even so, much of the time I still feel like a hypocrite and a failure as a mother. I soon began noticing that I wasn't the only one who felt this way. Most moms I ran into had similar feelings and insecurities. I couldn't figure it out. These were awesome moms who were intentional about raising godly children. They were careful about their children's media choices, took them to church every Sunday, and were growing in their own personal relationship with the Lord. Why did we all feel like such failures as mothers?

One morning I asked the Lord this question, and He really surprised me with His answer: *Because it is when you feel like a failure that you turn to Me and ask for help.* God was right. (Go figure.) No matter how creatively I correct, or how much I try to protect my kids, or how diligent I am to teach them, ultimately I will fail in my own strength. Only God can reach the spirits of our children, and we open the door for Him to touch their hearts when we bring our children before Him in prayer.

From that day on, I determined that I would not let the weight of failure burden me. Instead, I will let that be a reminder to me that I must roll off that pressure onto the Lord through prayer. Hebrews 4:16 says, "Let us then with confidence draw near to the throne of grace, that we may receive mercy and find grace to help in time of need." I have to accept that, no matter how hard I try, I still can't do this on my own. I need to ask for God's help.

I have also learned that I need to ask for other people's help. I don't know if it is pride or embarrassment or the desire to present a self-sufficient image, but I have the hardest time asking other people for help. I would much rather give help than receive it. But in this case, it isn't necessarily better to give than receive. We must also learn to receive.

Acts 2:44–45 says, "Now all who believed were together, and had all things in common, and sold their possessions and goods, and divided them among all, as anyone had need" (NKJV). It appears to me in these verses about the early church that as believers we are called to work together and share and help one another. Do you have a need? Of course you do. You probably need more sleep, for one. How about someone to simply listen? That's what the body of Christ is for.

Asking for help is one of the best things you can do to take care of the "me" in mommy. We ALL need help, and we don't have to feel guilty about asking. Soliciting help from others (who are often more willing to help than we realize) is a win-win solution. The person being asked to help wins by getting to act like Jesus, the model Servant. Our family wins because they experience a generous touch from hands other than just moms. And we win because we desperately needed help and we got it!

This week I want you to try asking for help. See if you can find a way in this next Rest Stop.

Ask for Help—Rest Stop
Help! I Need Help

Most of us know when we are "close to the edge" emotionally. Whether that's just an angry blowup or a more serious emotional breakdown, learn to recognize your own tendencies, and break the cycle of "going over the edge." Have a strategy in place, already planned, and put it into action. Whether that's a night away from the house while Dad makes sure the homework is complete, calling a friend and asking for prayer, or scheduling a counseling appointment with your pastor—whatever spells relief for you, have it readily in mind as a firm plan and put it into action when you feel yourself near the edge. It is a sign of wisdom, not a sign of weakness to ask for help!

 ## Ask God for Help

When you feel like you've failed miserably, ask God for a "do-over." If you aren't familiar with this phrase, it's one of our favorites at the Cauble household. When you are in the diving competition and your foot slips off the board, sometimes the judges will grant you a special grace—a "do-over."

Our loving heavenly Father fully understands our weaknesses and human frailties. Hebrews 4:15 says, "For we do not have a high priest who is unable to sympathize with our weaknesses, but one who in every respect has been tempted as we are, yet without sin." Hebrews 8:12 says, "Whatever failures or difficulties come, each morning—they suddenly become in the past! The apostle Paul tells us, "For I will be merciful toward their iniquities, and I will remember their sins no more." And Lamentations 3:22–23 says, You can have a fresh start. "The steadfast love of the LORD never ceases; his mercies never come to an end; they are new every morning; great is your faithfulness!"

Ask the Lord to make His mercies abundant—which means letting go of "what ifs," "if onlys," and "whys"—in general. Accept His abundant mercy and grace, give yourself a break from guilt and shame, and receive His provision for the day (and season) ahead.

 ## Ask Your Husband for Help

Your only real break may be when Dad releases you and takes over. Don't be afraid to help your husband understand your need for his voice and his help during the evenings with things like discipline, household chores, and homework.

Perhaps you could select one day each month where the evening is "Mom's Night Out," and arrange for Dad to watch the kids. You can do different things with your night. One month, for instance, could be scrapbooking night. Another month could be Bunco night at a friend's. The next month, movie night, and so on.

Ask Family and Friends for Help

Ask a friend to help you spot unrealistic expectations that may be causing feelings of failure. Have a good friend review your goals and to-do lists and help you be realistic about whatever season you are currently dealing with. Prioritize your goals, understanding that many of them will have to be put off until other seasons come. Your house will not be as clean as you like during the preschool years. You can't be at every soccer game for your ten-year-old when you still have two in diapers. Setting realistic expectations and having everyone in the house be realistic can be very releasing to stress and anxiety.

If you are feeling overwhelmed and never have time to spend any time alone with your husband, and you can't afford a baby-sitter—what's a mom to do? Turn to a friend! Find help by swapping out an evening with another couple so each couple can have some time alone. Be creative! For example, one day, you go to her house and fix dinner for both families while she and her husband go out. The next week, she does the same for you. Doing this means longer date nights—you might not be able to afford a sitter from 5:00 to 10:00 p.m., but you can drop the kids off at 5:00 and pick them up at 10:00 from a friend's house.

Think long and hard before moving away from grandparents, even if your husband is offered a job making a lot more money. There is a place in every child that only a grandparent's love and wisdom can fill. It is hard to put a monetary value on the influence of a grandparent.

If you are unmarried, pray for the Lord to send a friend, a family, or a college student to help you carry the load. Psalm 68:6 says, "God sets the solitary in families" (NKJV). He can work this either way, by placing you and your children within a surrogate family for support and friendship or by placing a single person within your family for the same benefit.

Everything is easier with a friend. Isolation is a strong tool of the enemy on every front. Find a friend in a similar season of life or one who has passed through your season, and be brave enough to open up to her about your difficulties. Ask your pastor to help you find a mentor. Titus 2:3–5 exhorts older women to teach the younger women. Whichever category you fall into, you need to be involved in helping another woman cope with life and life situations.

Look for a friend who isn't afraid to tell you, "Stop feeling sorry for yourself." Someone you can count on for a biblical, practical perspective, someone you can whine to without feeling judged, etc.

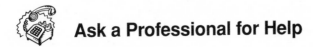 ## Ask a Professional for Help

If you are suffering from depression or feel overwhelmed, seek Christian counseling and/or medical treatment. If your doctor permits, medications and herbal remedies can bring your life back in balance and give you coping mechanisms you may be currently lacking.

Postpartum depression can take you off guard, sometimes showing up overnight as hormones rage. Seek help from your doctor, community programs, or local pastors and counselors to help you cope with feelings of depression and overload.

I would strongly recommend every woman go through Beth Moore's Bible study, *Breaking Free*.[17] Whether your challenges are big or small, you will get so much out of this study! And if you deal with guilt and the stress that comes from the self-imposed bondage it brings, this will help you break free and change your perspective. Ask the Lord if there is a root of bitterness or unforgiveness in your heart.

If you suspect your emotional struggle and feeling of being overwhelmed is rooted in a past event in your life—such as an abortion, sexual abuse, physical abuse, poor self-esteem, or current abuse by your husband—seek counseling immediately. Health and wholeness are on the other side, and the Lord wants to see you come to wellness. Many churches offer free counseling. There are also social agencies that offer support groups and counseling on many of these issues.

 Ask Me for Help

I want to help you help yourself so you can help others. Please join me in the next chapter where I suggest a way for us to continue this friendship on a daily basis and for you to follow through on some of the promptings of the Spirit you've felt while reading this book.

23

Personal Mom Coaching

$\mathcal{T}$oo often we read a book, nod our heads in agreement, purpose in our hearts to do better, try harder, be different, and really change this time, only to turn the last page, close the book, and lay it down somewhere alongside our best intentions. We want to implement the new things (or old things) we've learned but life starts too early in the morning, or at the same time our children are bickering, or after we've dropped into bed and given our husbands a kiss (or the exhausted kiss-off.) Our hearts are in the right place but our bodies are usually somewhere looking for a nap or a good cup of coffee.

We head off in the right direction, yet very quickly stumble and fall over the demands of the day without the energy to pull ourselves up by the bootstraps. We need help! A really wise man once said, "Two are better than one, because they have a good reward for their toil For if they fall, one will lift up his fellow. But woe to him who is alone when he falls and has not another to lift him up!" (Ecclesiastes 4:9–10 ESV)

I would like to be that friend for you. May I walk beside you on this road to taking care of the "Me" in Mommy? It is always more fun to share an experience with a friend. Who wants to go on a journey by themselves when they can have someone take the trip with them? If that sounds like fun to you then meet me at www.LisaWhelchel.com, click on the "Personal Mom Coach" heading, and I'll be there waiting.

Okay, so I'll virtually be there waiting, but we can still have a good time and support one another. Here's how it works. Once you're inside the special web section designed especially for my *Taking Care of the Me in Mommy* friends, we'll start building some good habits.

We could start our journey together emphasizing any of the three core areas of *Spirit, Body,* or *Soul.* I recommend that as we strive to become better moms we start with our spirit. Choose one area to focus on your spiritual walk: Prayer, Bible Reading, Journaling or Worship. They say it takes three weeks to establish a habit. So, for the next twenty-one days you will receive an email from me each morning. Within that email will be a friendly reminder, a word of encouragement, a practical tip and a prayer.

Because we not only need support, we also need someone with enough tough love to hold us accountable for the commitment we've made; I'm also going to include a special "We did it!" link within the email. I use the pronoun "we" to remind you that you are not alone on this journey. We are in this together, and more importantly it is God who will supply you with the strength you need to accomplish your goals.

Hebrews 10:24 says, "And let us consider how to stir up one another to love and good works." It is not my intention to nag you or make you feel guilty if you just aren't able to accomplish your goal for the day, but I do want to stir you up a bit. By including the "We did it!" link, I'm hoping to give you just that added incentive to find time for yourself, even if some days it is simply for the thrill of being able to click that link and send the announcement of your "good works" so I may rejoice with you. At the end of twenty-one days you not only will have established a wonderful habit, but you will also receive a multimedia celebration "Congratulations!" card from me. (Whoo-hoo!)

Then we will tackle another area. This time why don't you choose something from the *Body* or *Soul* areas? Have you had your annual female check up? If not, then choose the "Do Something For Yourself" category on the website and expect me to nag, I mean gently remind you, every morning in your computer Inbox until you've made the appointment and can click the "We did it!" link. (Remember, not only are you taking care of your health but you are also guaranteed an hour of peace and quiet in the waiting room reading magazines.)

We can keep this friendship up for as long as you are willing to work on habits that will minister to you so you can better minister to your family. The Apostle Paul writes to his friends in Rome that he desires to see them and "be helped on my journey there by you, once I have enjoyed your company for awhile" (Romans 15:24 ESV). That's how I feel! I'm really looking forward to our new online friendship and, hopefully, helping you along the way on your journey. God Speed.

Appendix 1
How to Find a Baby-Sitter

Many of the ideas in this book require finding someone else to take care of your children while you take care of yourself. This is especially difficult if you are not married, your husband is often unavailable, or you don't live near your parents. I've put together this little appendix, in the style of a Rest Stop to point you in a handful of directions designed to help you find trustworthy and reliable baby-sitters.

❖ As you begin searching for a baby-sitter, think through what you need and specifically what you are looking for. If you have a baby or a toddler, you may want to look for an adult who has had plenty of personal experience with younger children. Preschoolers may enjoy a middle schooler with plenty of energy and enthusiasm for playing with them. Older children may prefer a high school student to look up to and yet one who is not too old to join them in some of their favorite activities.

❖ What kind of time frame are you looking at? Do you mostly want a baby-sitter who can come over occasionally during the day while you tackle some domestic chores? Are you looking for a baby-sitter to get the kids down at night while you and your hubby enjoy date night? Can you offer someone a consistent job, say once a week, or three afternoons a week?

❖ How much can you afford to pay? Ask other parents what the going rate for a baby-sitter is these days. Is it more for each additional child?

❖ Do you need a baby-sitter who can drive or whose parents can bring them and pick them up?

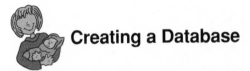 ## Creating a Database

The goal is to collect as many names of baby-sitters you can depend on as possible. Create a database and constantly be on the lookout for more sitters. You can never have too long a list. Here are a few places to look:

❖ Think through your relatives. Would any of them be willing and available to baby-sit? Do any of them have children old enough to baby-sit if you brought them over to their house?

❖ Ask other parents of children your age for referrals. You may be surprised how many are willing to share this valuable information. (You may also be surprised at how many aren't so generous.)

❖ If you find a reliable sitter, ask her if she has a sister or other friends she recommends who could baby-sit if she is not available.

❖ Churches are great places to keep your eyes and ears open. I doubt you could call up a church at random and get them to give you a list of competent teenagers in their youth group. Still, you could visit your church's youth group one Wednesday night and scan the crowd for teenagers who might be interested. Do the same thing in the nursery department. Many of the volunteers are there because they love kids and might be looking for a way to make a bit of extra money. It doesn't hurt to ask.

❖ Contact scout troops, clubs, and YWCA's. Ask leaders if there are any young people who are taking courses in baby-sitting or earning badges in child care whom they would recommend and be willing to pass along your phone number and information.

❖ Many local colleges and universities have lists already made up of students looking for baby-sitting jobs. Call the school office to inquire about an existing list. You may even want to ask to be connected to the education department. Most students seeking a degree in this area would love the opportunity to make a little extra money doing what they already love to do.

The Interview Process

I'm assuming if you are reading this book you have children and you've already hired your fair share of baby-sitters. (If not, then I'm very glad you are reading this book, because it is definitely time to hire a baby-sitter so you can do a little something for yourself!) Even so, I've collected a list of questions you may want to ask a potential baby-sitter. Keep in mind that you are not asking many of these questions to get an answer as much as to get a "feel" for the baby-sitter—you know, that mother's intuition tool.

❖ How old are you? (If appropriate)

❖ Where do you live? (Will your mother be at home?)

❖ How long have you been baby-sitting/What is your baby-sitting experience?

❖ Have you ever cared for children the ages of my children? When and for how long?

❖ Have you ever had first-aid/CPR training? Have you ever prepared simple meals for children when you were baby-sitting? What kinds of things did you make?

❖ What would you do if the baby kept on crying and you knew he wasn't hungry or wet?

❖ What would you do if the children refused to do what you asked them to do?

❖ What kinds of activities do you like to do with children?

❖ What do you enjoy most about baby-sitting?

❖ How late can you sit on weeknights? On weekends? In the summer?

❖ Will you need to be picked up? Can you have someone come get you if my children are already in bed?

❖ What do you charge?

❖ Could you give me the names and phone numbers of two or three people for whom you have worked so I could call them?

When you call the references, don't be afraid to get specific and ask the tough questions. Did the sitter arrive on time? Has she ever canceled at the last minute? Were the children peaceful when you returned? Do your children look forward to her coming over? In what shape does she leave the house? Do you feel confident she could handle kids my children's ages?

You may want to consider a trial run. The next time you need to get a few things done around the house, invite the sitter over. Pay her and then do your thing, checking in periodically to see how she's interacting with your child and how your child is responding to her.

Before You Leave

I highly recommend you have a handful of lists ready to go over and leave with your baby-sitter. It is also a good idea to have your sitter arrive at least thirty minutes earlier than you need to leave. This will give you time to run through these lists and any last-minute instructions. You will also have time to finish getting ready in peace while your child is getting acclimated to the sitter. Consider preparing the following lists to be printed out every time you leave:

Emergency Information

❖ Where you will be and how to reach you. (Cell phone or name and phone number of restaurant, friend's house, etc.)

❖ An emergency contact in case you can't be reached

❖ A medical release and copy of insurance card

❖ Neighbors' phone numbers

❖ Relatives' phone numbers

❖ Physician's phone numbers

❖ Poison Control number

❖ Don't forget to include your own phone number and address on this list.

❖ List any allergies or special emergency information regarding your children.

 # Things to Know

You know where everything is in your house and how everything works, but your sitter doesn't. Take time one afternoon to write up a document explaining "how to live" in your house for an evening.

❖ Where to find:

- All utensils needed to cook a meal for your children

- Extra sheets (in case of accidents)

- Extra diapers and other baby supplies

- Cleaning supplies (in case of accidents or extremely ambitious sitters)

- First-aid kit and children's medicines (along with instruction when to administer and how much)

- Fire extinguisher (make sure she knows how to use it)

- Extra toilet paper

- Flashlights

- Towels

❖ Children's preferences:

- Favorite toys

- Favorite books

- Bedtime routines

- Any security blankets or items

- Does your child have any special words that she should know how to interpret?

❖ How to use your:

  - Television/cable unit

  - DVD or VHS player

  - Oven

  - Baby monitors

  - Thermostat

  - Microwave

❖ Schedules:

  - Meal times

  - Bath times

  - Bed times

  - Play times

  - Nap times

  - Any other routines or rituals

 **House Rules**

I don't know about your kids, but mine tried to get away with stuff with the baby-sitter that they would never attempt with me. You may want to leave a list of house rules and other information that would help keep order while you are gone.

- ❖ Be honest about your children. Do they have a propensity for dangerous curiosity, stretching the truth, hitting siblings, tying up baby-sitters?

- ❖ Spell out television rules—what is allowed and what isn't allowed.

- ❖ What are the rules regarding the computer?

- ❖ Are they allowed to eat in between meal snacks? If so, what kind?

- ❖ How late are they allowed to stay up? Can they read in their beds?

- ❖ Leave suggestions for correction you feel is acceptable. Do you feel comfortable using time-outs? Sending your children to their rooms? When should they call you for advice on how to handle disciplinary situations?

- ❖ Warn your sitter about issues you know your children are dealing with. Do you have a baby who is fascinated with the stairs? A preschooler who likes to "carry" the baby around? An older child who likes to make prank calls?

- ❖ Don't be afraid to write out a few expectations for your sitter. How do you feel about her using the phone? Eating your food? Having a friend over? Chatting on your computer? Television watching? Doing homework? Do any of these rules change after the children are all in bed?

- ❖ Do you expect her to clean up the kitchen and straighten up the family room before you return?

 **Now Leave Already**

You've done all you can do; now kiss your child, grab your purse, head out the door, and don't look back. Remember, this is actually as good for your child as it is for you. They need to know that you leave but you always come back. It is important that they learn to relate to and obey other authority figures in their lives. Believe it or not, they are going to learn some good things from this baby-sitter that they simply can't learn from you.

Walk out the door cheerfully and with confidence. If you are feeling anxious about leaving your child, don't let them know that. They will take that piece of information and play it for all it's worth. Take the time before you leave to explain where you are going, when you will be back, and what will happen in the meantime. After you've done that, feel good about this decision you've made to do something for yourself so you can return refreshed and ready to give some more.

If your child cries or clings as you are heading out the door, keep walking. It is actually healthier for them to learn how to be without you occasionally than it is to become so dependent on you that they are incapable of any self-actualization. Tell your sitter to call you if they don't calm down after fifteen minutes. At that time, you can calmly and confidently reassure your child that he or she is okay and you will be home soon. Otherwise, don't call home and interrupt the fun time they are probably already having.

Keep the goal in mind. You are doing something for yourself so you can ultimately be an even better mother when you return. Your child is too young to understand that, in the long run, he or she would rather have a mother who is gone occasionally rejuvenating her juices, than one who never leaves and gets burned out and worn down.

Trust me, no matter how much you need the break, you are actually going to miss those little buggers when you are gone, and when you return you will love your job as mommy even more than before you left. So go, get filled up so you can give some more.

Appendix 2
How to Get a Babysitter for Free (or almost free!)

Even with help finding a baby-sitter, money is still often the main obstacle to overcome. When my children were little, I was a stay-at-home mom living on my pastor husband's salary. We just didn't have much disposable income for baby-sitters. Thankfully, I was rich with good friends. Whether you have a lot or a little money, a ton of friends or a handful of acquaintances, I want to help you find the best kind of baby-sitters—friends who are free!

 Creative Solutions

❖ Find another mom with children your age. Encourage each other to feel free to call whenever you need to run an errand, go out with hubby, or just need a break. Drop your children off at her house when you go out and she'll drop hers off at yours when she is going somewhere. No need to keep track of whose turn it is—that's just what friends are for.

❖ Do you have a friend or two whom you would like to meet for coffee, Bible study, or scrapbooking once a week? Hire a sitter and split the cost.

❖ Think of activities with your friends or dates where you can bring your children along. You can still enjoy alone time with your husband or time to talk with your girlfriend while your children play at the park, or read books in a bookstore, or play in the ball house at Chuck E. Cheese's® pizza restaurant.

❖ One Christmas season, I really needed time to shop, bake, wrap gifts, clean my house for parties, and yet accomplished a handful of other activities that would be a whole lot easier without my children around. So, I arranged for a Christmas co-op. For the month of December, every Friday, instead of having our regular MomTime meeting, we brought all of the children over to one mom's house and one other mom stayed to help. That meant six moms went shopping while two moms watched twelve children who weren't in school. As it turned out, each mom had three full days alone for one day of total exhaustion. It wasn't a bad trade-off.

 ## How to Start a Baby-Sitting Co-op

Do-It-Yourself

A baby-sitting co-op is a group of moms who always have a baby-sitter available and never have to spend any money for it. Sound too good to be true? Well, it is not only possible, but it is actually very easy to put together. Here's how to get started:

❖ You can start with as few as three moms.

❖ The more moms the better, so immediately begin inviting more moms to join. Put fliers in mailboxes, post one on the church bulletin board, talk about it in your MOPS group, etc. Believe me, word will spread like wildfire.

❖ Print up some fun "Baby Bucks" or buy tokens from the teacher supply store or raffle tickets from the party store.

❖ Designate an amount each "Baby Buck" is worth. For instance, one "buck" is worth one hour of baby-sitting for one or two children, two "bucks" for three or more.

❖ As soon as a mom signs up by adding their name, address, availability, children's ages, phone number, and e-mail, to the co-op directory she earns three "bucks" to begin.

❖ As long as you have some "bucks," you can call a mom in the directory and ask if they are available to baby-sit. Simply pay her with your "bucks" and then she'll have more to spend when she needs a baby-sitter.

❖ If you need to earn some more "bucks," send out an e-mail expressing your interest and availability. I can't imagine you will have any trouble finding a few takers.

❖ Encourage the moms to actively spread the word to friends they trust and can confidently recommend so there are plenty of opportunities to earn (and spend) more "Baby Bucks."

Get Step-by-Step Instructions and Tools

If you need a bit more hand-holding, then I would suggest you immediately log on to www.Amazon.com and purchase the book, *Smart Mom's Baby-Sitting Co-Op Handbook: How We Solved the Baby-Sitter Puzzle* by Gary Myers. This book utilizes a rotating secretary and group organizer to keep track of a point system rather than something tangible to change hands like "Baby Bucks." This also has the added advantage of giving moms who most need to earn points the first opportunity to accept baby-sitting opportunities. Between the tools and instructions, you barely even have to think about how to get your baby-sitting co-op off the ground.

 **Even More Help**

If you really want to go high-tech, log onto www.babysitterexchange.com. For a small fee, this software program and Web site will also do all of the secretarial work for you. You really don't even have to think if you go this route. This option also has a few nice checks-and-balances to make sure every family is recommended and confirmed by at least two existing members.

Aren't you getting excited? Just think. You can leave your children in the homes of families you trust without feeling guilty about paying them back or spending money out of the grocery money. By taking a little time up front, you will be able to set up a system to actually make it possible to take advantage of some of the suggestions in this book to take better care of yourself. Isn't God good?

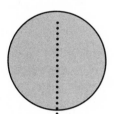

Notes

1. John Piper, *Desiring God: Meditations of a Christian Hedonist.* (Sisters, OR.: Multnomah Books, 1996).

2. Spiros Zodhiates, *The Complete Word Study Dictionary: New Testament* (Chattanooga, TN.: AMG, 2000, c1992, c1993), electronic ed. (G4151), s.v. "Spirit."

3. Ibid., s.v. "Body."

4. K. S. Wuest, *Wuest's Word Studies from the Greek New Testament: For the English Reader* (Grand Rapids, MI.: Eerdmans, 1997, c1984), s.v. "Soul."

5. "Let the Peace of God Reign" © Darlene Zschech.

6. Lisa Whelchel, *The Facts of Life and Other Lessons My Father Taught Me* (Sisters, OR.: Multnomah Books, 2003).

7. Lisa Whelchel, *The Busy Mom's Guide to Prayer: A Guided Prayer Journal* (West Monroe, LA.: Howard, 2005).

8. Beth Moore, *A Heart Like His* (Nashville: Broadman and Holman, 1999); Beth Moore, *A Woman's Heart: God's Dwelling Place* (Nashville, TN.: LifeWay Christian Resources, 1995).

9. Lisa Whelchel, *Creative Correction* (Wheaton, IL.: Tyndale, 2000).

10. Lisa Whelchel, *Creative Correction: The Bible Study* (Nashville, TN.: LifeWay Christian Resources, 2005).

11. "Who Can Satisfy My Soul?" © Dennis Jernigan; 1989 Shepherd's Heart Music, Inc.

12. Lisa Whelchel, *Mom Time Journal*, available at www.LisaWhelchel.com.

13. Kathryn Hammer, *And How Are We Feeling Today?* (Chicago: Contemporary Books, 1993). Available at http://ccpintprod.mhedu.com/wa/permissions.htm.

14. Richard Foster, *Celebration of Discipline: The Path to Spiritual Growth* (New York, NY.: Harper and Row, 1978).

15. Karen Ehman, *Homespun Gifts from the Heart* (Grand Rapids, MI.: Fleming H. Revell, 2003).

16. Randy Alcorn, *Money, Possessions, and Eternity* (Wheaton, IL.: Tyndale, 2003).

17. Beth Moore, *Breaking Free* (Nashville, TN.: Broadman and Holman, 2000).